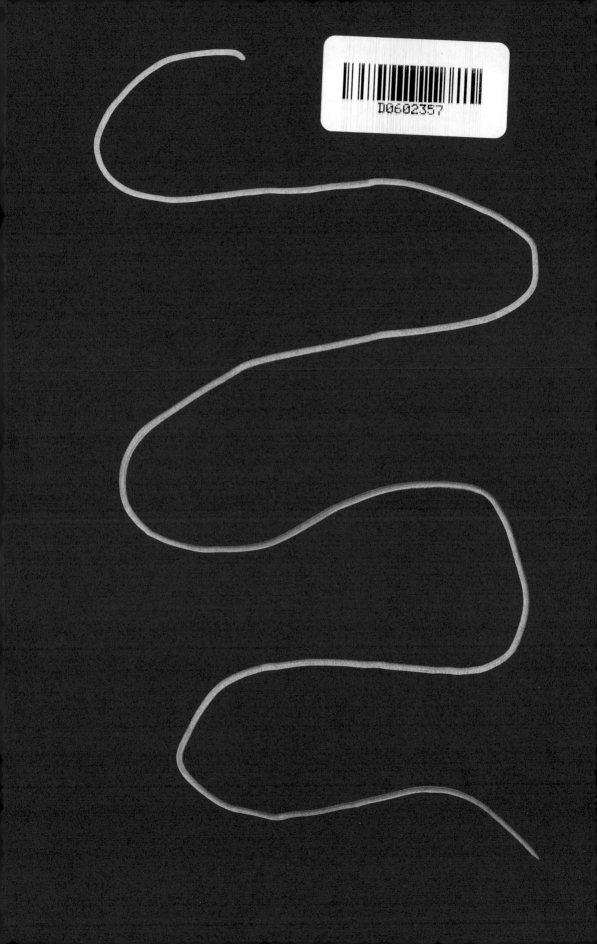

Culinary Excursions through Germany

Wolfgang W. Reichert

Culinary Excursions through Germany

SIGLOCH
EDITION

Frontispice, page 2: German congeniality not only can be found around the domestic dinner table but many German restaurant interiors exude German "Gemütlichkeit" and reflect local traditions and customs. The culinary artistry of the chef, the excellent wines and the smooth beer as well as the friendly service combine to make the guests feel like a king.

The recipes of this book have been selected and edited from the individual German-language editions of the "Kulinarische Streifzüge" (Culinary Excursions) series by Sigloch Edition, Künzelsau, by the following authors:

Frank Gerhard (Bavaria, Frankonia, Frisia, Hesse, Swabia)
Roland Gööck (Westphalia)
Wolfgang von Gropper (Palatinate)
Karin Iden (Lower Saxony)
Georg Richter (Baden)
Hannes Schmitz (Rhineland)

The recipe photographs beginning on page 14 were taken by Hans Joachim Döbbelin

These "Culinary Excursions through Germany" perhaps deserve a sub-title which might aptly be called "The truth about German cooking", as there are few areas pertaining to German mores and life-styles that suffer from so many misconceptions among foreigners than the culinary and nutritional habits within the various regions of Germany.

It was our desire not only to rectify these misconceptions but to take our Anglo-Saxon readership on an excursion through a different and exciting culinary world inside the ethnic sub-divisions of post-war Germany.

It is obvious that it is virtually impossible to justify the ambitious title of the book, since only a limited number of recipes could be selected from an over-powering multitude of possibilities.

But when choosing the present collection, careful attention was paid to select only recipes that represent meals as they appear at family dinners throughout the nation – recipes that can be duplicated by homemakers elsewhere with ease and with the devotion of the curious. The world is already filled with books on haute-cuisine, books that usually stay in bookshelves forever. We didn't want to add another one to this category.

We have not only consulted Grandma's cookbooks but have also looked over the shoulders of many housewives and particularly into the pots and pans of many well-known chefs in some of these charming and attractive country inns that have made their mark on the German culinary scene in the post-war decades with a delectable, esthetic, appetizing and relatively light, yet characteristically German fare.

May these culinary excursions, seasoned with a little bit of history and story-telling, inspire our readers to attempt and savor these recipes to their hearts', their guests' and their loved ones' content.

Author and Publishers

Introduction

There has always been a question as to whether a real and clearly definable German national cuisine exists, or, for that matter, any national cuisine.

The answer, at least as far as Western countries are concerned, must be an ambivalent one. Surely, we have come to accept certain "national dishes" in one country or the other as typical for the respective country, but that does not make their entire spectrum of recipes typical for any given country. On the contrary, in studying international cookbooks one will always be surprised to find the same or similar recipes in these "national" cookbooks, recipes which are claimed by the respective authors to be typical for the country in question. As a matter of fact, the great majority of well-known recipes are shared by most nations and their origin lies deeply buried in the history of mankind itself. There has been so much "cross-pollination" in this field and we would like to retrace some of these influences as they pertain to the German culinary history.

Western civilization and all of its values, which we still treasure today, is based on two nations and three major cities: ancient Greece, with Athens as its major cultural center, laid the foundation for Western philosophy, ethics and moral values, stressing the importance of the individual in society and the political environment. Ancient Rome, building on Greek philosophies, codified moral values and human behavior into legal codes, gave the Western world Roman law on which the legal codes of many Western countries are still based today, including that of Germany. The third column of Western civilization is the city of Jerusalem. It is the birthplace not only of the Christian faith – it also gave the Western civilization a monotheistic religion, a religion based on the moral values of Judaism and on influences emanating from early Greek philosophies.

One of the greatest physical pleasures among the citizens of the middle classes and of the aristocracy in ancient Rome was eating and the refinement of foods. Cooking was developed to a fine art through the addition of a wide variety of spices and herbs. The first cookbooks appeared, written by gourmets, philosophers and even generals. Famous among these was Marcus Gavius Apicius who lived under Emperor Tiberius from 42 BC to 37 AD; then there were Plinius and his father, Plinius the Elder, and field marshal Licinius Lucullus, perhaps the most well-known Roman gourmet of all times. Let us just look at one of Apicius' recipes for a moment: "Pepper, pine seeds, honey and rue – mix with raisin wine and milk, boil the mixture and, together with a few eggs, form dumplings, sprinkle with honey and serve."

As the Roman Empire expanded it was inevitable not to introduce some of their culinary achievements, spices and ingredients into the countries they had conquered. There were not only Roman legionaries in Germany but also Roman settlers with sizeable landholdings and German servants as well as a very affluent German upper class. The Roman rule over part of the Germanic tribes lasted for four centuries, not unlike the times they spent in France and Britain. While the Roman historian Tacitus praised the Germans' character as an example of natural behavior and virtue, compared to his already decadent compatriots, he had this to say about their eating habits: "Their food is simple: wild fruits, fresh venison and sour milk. They satisfy their hunger without specially preparing their food and without using any spices."

That was probably as arrogant a remark as it was ignorant. Had Mr. Tacitus been able to see for himself, he would have discovered that venison was mostly reserved for the privileged classes and that many families had their own grist mill for preparing their daily flour and porridge needs. He could have also observed agriculture on a high level and animal husbandry, including the fattening of pigs. He probably ate ham in Rome without knowing it was imported from Germany, as cheese also was.

There were constant contacts and intermingling. The Roman army had conscripted and incorporated great numbers of Germanic legions into their ranks. Emperor Constantin (Flavius Valerius Constantinus) who, as first Roman Emperor had converted to the Christian faith in the fourth century, had ruled the Roman Empire for some time from

The Romans brought many culinary inspirations to "Germania" during their occupation and even engaged in viniculture. The picture shows the gravestone of a wine trader in the shape of a Roman barge in Neumagen near Trier on the Moselle River (3rd century AD).

Trevira (today the city of Trier on the Moselle River), before ruling it from the new capital of Constantinople when the East Roman Empire started to show signs of deterioration.

Is it any wonder that eating habits in "Germania" had undergone rather substantial changes during and after Roman rule? It wasn't a one-way street, however. As happened so frequently in history, the conquerors did not leave the conquered entirely unscathed for they, too, had come to like certain foods in the occupied territories which they took back to Rome to enrich Roman fare, ham being one of them.

With the fall of the Roman Empire this entire, rather comfortable life in the villas in the countryside and the teeming towns along the Rhine, where natives and legionaries, traders from Greece and jugglers from Asia Minor mingled, had come to an end once and for all. The Franks had taken over the whole region including the Moselle area after a number of peremptory incursions during the fifth century from areas to the East. It took a few centuries until the Franks had come to an arrangement with Celts, Romans who had chosen to stay, with Frisians in the North, Saxons in the East, Alemanics in the South and last but not least, Christians and pagans alike.

New stature and wealth came to the Western areas under a King and Emperor who was the ruler of all Franks, including the largest part of what is France today – his Latin name: Carolus Magnus, his French name: Charlemagne and his German name: Karl der Große. He was enthroned as Roman Emperor in the city of Aachen with the blessings of Pope Leo III in 800 AD. It meant the renewal of the Western Roman Empire in which the Christian-Roman traditions were joined with the German nation. His rule extended over

large portions of Europe, all the way to the Ebro River in Spain.

It also marks the beginning of the Middle Ages. Needless to say that there was brisk trading within the vast and diverse areas of the Carolingian Empire. Again, the culinary arts received further impetus, refinement and diversification.

It was mostly the nobility and the affluent, but sparse, upper class that profited indeed from the vastly expanding horizons and the beginning of the trade routes to the East. Large portions of the populace ate what was available in their immediate area and made the most of it. Refinements and changes came slowly over the centuries and they frequently were merely making the local fare more appetizing and appealing. Definite regional characteristics in food and ingredients had established themselves – the beginnings of regional cuisines – where simple, basic staples were used in a limited number of variations. Since most people were merely able to eke out a bare living – and sometimes less than that – it is a wonder that ingenuity was able to do so much with so little.

Charlemagne's Empire broke up after his death due to the resulting internecine quarreling of his sons over his vast heritage. An interlude followed, characterized by short-lived royal and imperial reigns until the Staufer dynasty made its mark, primarily on the Germanic areas and Italy. At the height of their power their territory extended all the way to Sicily. Their rule partly coincides with one of the phenomena of European history, one that excited both the masses as well as the nobility – the Crusades. There were seven Crusades altogether from 1096 to 1270 with the avowed aim to liberate the Holy Sites, mainly Jerusalem, from the domination of the infidels. They were mostly French, German and English knights that led the Crusades.

But what have the Crusades got to do with the culinary arts? A great deal as we are to learn. The knights – they were the only educated people among the Crusade participants – soon found exciting foods and spices along their routes to North Africa and Palestine besides the booty of ransacked cities on the way. Their palates must have been tickled by all the new and exotic odors and tastes of hitherto unknown herbs and spices which they eventually brought or had sent home.

The quest for Near and Far Eastern spices had just been stimulated. What couldn't be taken by force had to be paid for. The time for the merchants and for the Eastern trade routes had come and many towns along these routes became very prosperous. It was that same quest for satisfying the human palate and to amass riches that would send off one Christopher Columbus to find a safer and easier route by sea to Western India. He did find what he called the "West Indies", but we know where he really landed, don't we!

Back to the merchants and overland trade routes. Fortunes were made by enterprising merchants who could afford to outfit trips to the East in the waning years of the Middle Ages and into the ascendancy of the exciting Age of the Renaissance.

The Renaissance – often called the maker of modern man – despite its French name actually had its beginnings in Italy or, to be more precise, in the city states of Rome, Venice and, towering above all others: Florence, under the aegis of the Medici family. The Renaissance was supposed to be the rebirth of the new-gleaned wisdom of buried Greece and Rome. Now, the Middle Ages in retrospect appeared as dark and barbarous times. The explosion of knowledge and enlightenment within a century spread to most of the rest of Europe.

Why delve into the Renaissance at length in a cookbook? Because the Renaissance also brought on a revolution in the culinary arts as some of the wealth and knowledge spread to the general populace. The refinement and the art of preparing foods reached heights of sophistication no one could have dreamed of before. As Venice reached its pinnacle of power, its merchants brought spices and other exotic goods to the City of the Doges and distributed them over well-organized trade routes

Germany is famous for her many medieval castles. Here, Katz Castle, surrounded by vineyards, has been beckoning Rhine River sailors for centuries. A little further upstream beautiful Loreley used to sing her seductive songs from atop a big rock in the river.

throughout Europe – a Europe that was thirsting for luxuries. No other period in European history has influenced people more and wrought so many changes in such a short time.

And it is during the Renaissance that an event took place, which is considered an established part of cultural history and which has come to be accepted as the origin of the "refined" French cuisine. In 1533, Catherine de Medici travelled from Florence to France to marry the French Heir Apparent. Her retinue included a few Italian cooks and pastry bakers. Later, in the same century, Maria de Medici came to France as the bride of Henry IV. Both women were credited not only with the introduction of the new Italian way of cooking but also with introducing new vegetables such as savoy cabbage, artichokes, broccoli and others. Their refined style de cuisine was to be codified in 1655 by Pierre de la Varenne and to be expanded subsequently by such culinary geniuses as La Reynière or Brillat-Savarin, the latter in the last century.

Whether we like it or not, we have to acknowledge the fact that wars also greatly contributed to the spread of culinary knowledge, especially in a centrally located country like Germany. When France became an absolutist monarchy under Louis XIV (1638–1715) and Germany was a weak conglomeration of small fiefdoms, Southwest Germany was frequently overrun by the French army who ransacked and ransomed German cities, staying for a while and leaving behind some of their own cooking innovations and specialties.

Even more profound was the impact of Napoleon and his conquests all over Europe at the end of the 18th and the beginning of the 19th centuries, because French culture and everything else French became very fashionable among European society. While there is no denying the overwhelming influence of the French cuisine on the art of cooking of today, there is also the simple truth that many of the recipes of such French culinary giants are shunned by the average housewife as she considers many of them too sophisticated, in fact too difficult to reproduce.

And what about German cuisine? Is there such a thing? We feel the German cuisine is a conglomerate of regional recipes, many of which have attained national stature. German cuisine, unknown to many foreigners, offers a tremendous spectrum of regional recipes from very distinctly different ethnic groups that had their own history before being melded into the German nation. And no one will deny that recipes have changed, as they always will, over the centuries. It was either through inter-marriages of the European nobility, the spread of mercantilism, the influence of monasteries on the culinary and brewing sciences, invading armies from all sides and, more recently, through wide-spread international exposure and traveling.

France is said to offer several hundred types of cheeses, but Germany prides itself on being able to offer several hundred types of excellent sausages and over a hundred different types of bread, some of them being the most wholesome and healthy to be found anywhere.

We have made every effort to collect 95 recipes from ten different German regions; from Southern German areas such as Baden, Bavaria, Swabia, Frankonia and the Palatinate, the central region of Hesse, the Western areas of the Rhineland and Westphalia, the North being represented by Lower Saxony and Frisia.

Our selection reflects the regional tastes and preferences as well as the geographical and climatic location of these areas. It also mirrors the advances of the past forty years – advances that have not altered the basic philosophies of German food and eating habits, namely that food has to be wholesome in the first place and that refinements are to accentuate the taste of the basic ingredients. Refinements and exotic ingredients should enhance the basic foods to meet that primary object. They are not a means in themselves.

Upper right: Germans love to quaff their beer or drink wine in the open air in summer time, as on Viktualienmarkt in Munich. – Below: Many farmers in the country still do their own slaughtering. The lucky ones still have their own smoke house for sausages and ham. Even bread-baking at home or in the communal brick oven bake house is still – or again – a wide-spread custom.

The German cuisine of today is a living, dynamic institution. There are few countries in the world that can offer such an even and high standard of foods in restaurants throughout the country, be it in cities or in villages. There is no search for substitutes and the stress is on quality. No one can be a chef unless he has learned the trade for at least three years under a master chef and at the same time gone to trade schools. Advanced chefs will attend one of several highly reputed Gastronomy Colleges. Many of the graduates can later be found as chefs in international hotels around the world. Being a composite of regional cooking, German cuisine has had a sufficiently broad basis for the development of a certain national character, still based on nutritional soundness; heartier than French and more versatile than Italian cooking.

We can only wish you fun and success with these recipes and, of course, "Guten Appetit!"

On Ingredients and Equivalents

Your author knows from first-hand experience how difficult it is for most people to switch from the metric to the British/American system of weights and measures and vice versa, and how utterly frustrating it is to compare certain foods and ingredients from one country to those of another. It is not only the difference in philosophy toward certain foods and their preparation, but ingredients do differ occasionally in potency, physical appearance and composition as well as reactivity and compatibility with one another.

In order to assure the same qualitative results as in the original recipes, the author painstakingly researched German and American manufacturers of similar products, consulted with nutritional research institutes at various universities and experimented himself, when in doubt, to make certain that, in the end, similar virtually became identical. For those of our readership who may be living in Germany, such as our friends from the American, British and Canadian Armed Forces, we have occasionally given a choice between a German and an American product. And, in a few cases, we have given a choice between *lard* and *shortening* for those cooks who would like to try the old, original composition despite the fact that lard is not found very frequently in German "larders" any more.

Vanilla in Germany is sold either in the shape of a thin natural stick in a glass vial or as vanilla-flavored sugar and not as an extract. The natural vanilla is very rarely used except, perhaps, for certain very specific recipes. We have given a choice between the vanilla-flavored sugar and vanilla extract in their proper relationship.

German housewives to a large degree prefer compressed *yeast* because the dry active yeast has not been available too long. Again, you will find the equivalents between compressed yeast and American dry active yeast.

Some of the recipes call for *unflavored gelatin,* and we did not recommend the German sheet gelatin because it is rather cumbersome to use. Instead we recommended Knox unflavored gelatin, a U.S. product. A good equivalent to be found in German stores is a white, granulated gelatin made by the Dr. Oetker company. Both products can be used interchangeably, envelope for envelope, despite their different net weights.

As for *flour,* we recommend an unbleached, all-purpose flour. As a general guideline, the German classification would be labelled as Type 405. Do not use instant flour at any time.

Double Acting *baking powder* is your best choice for our recipes. And, should you be living in Germany, why not buy Swiss or German *chocolates* for your cooking or baking needs. They seem to be so much more delicious, and there is a wide variety of them available from bitter through bitter-sweet to sweet milk chocolates and special ones for frosting, called "couvertures".

German housewives still prefer fresh vegetables and ingredients over canned or frozen ones. The numerous greengrocers and picturesque market scenes in small and large towns bear witness to his preference. The picture shows the Market Square in Lüneburg in front of the 1720 City Hall façade.

Apples in Morning Gown

Westphalia

When the first apples begin to ripen it is Apples-in-Morning-Gown time in Westphalia. And don't ask anyone where the name came from – you will not receive an answer since nobody knows. The raisin filling can be varied at will, for instance with cranberry or apricot jam or even with honey. Or you can make the "gown" from a yeast dough or a frozen pie crust. It's that easy!

For the dough:
5 oz. cottage cheese, uncreamed, unsalted (Quark in Germany)
6 tbsp. milk
6 tbsp. oil
6 tbsp. sugar
1 package vanilla-flavored sugar or 1 tsp. vanilla extract
1 pinch salt
2 1/2 cups flour
4 tsp. baking powder
For the filling:
8 medium-sized apples
7 oz. raisins (1 1/3 cups)
2–3 tbsp. confectioner's sugar
For glazing:
2 tbsp. water
1 egg yolk

With a spoon press cottage cheese through fine-meshed sieve, mix with milk, oil, sugar, vanilla and salt. Mix flour and baking powder, mix half the flour with cottage cheese mixture, then add other half to obtain smooth dough. With rolling pin roll dough abt. 3/16″ (4mm) thick, cut into 6″–8″ squares. Pare and core apples. Mix raisins with confectioner's sugar and fill apple cores. Place one apple on one square of dough, each, pull up dough corners crosswise and firmly press together. Mix water and yolk and brush on apples. Bake in oven 25 to 30 minutes at 375°–395°F (190°–200°C). They taste even sweeter with a glazing of confectioner's sugar and lemon juice.

Bavarian
Baked Meat Loaf

Bavaria

Perhaps the most popular Bavarian titbit is Leber-käs, lit. "liver cheese", although it contains neither. It actually consists of 80% beef and 20% pork. Bavarian butchers make it at least twice a day for the obligatory snacks in-between around 10 a.m. and 4 p.m. Connoisseurs know it tastes best while it is fresh and warm, whereas gourmets go for the crisp end pieces.

1 3/4 lbs. finely ground beef
7 oz. finely ground pork
9 oz. bacon, ground
salt
1 tbsp. + 1 tsp. ground mace (or pinch of nutmeg)
1 tbsp. + 1 tsp. ground black pepper
1 1/4 – 2 1/2 cups lukewarm water
2 tbsp. butter
1 onion, minced

Knead ground beef on wooden board till smooth, add ground pork, ground bacon and spices and mix thoroughly. While kneading add enough water to keep mixture smooth but not too thin. Spread butter evenly in roasting pan, evenly sprinkle onion in it. Form meat loaf and place in open pan, brush top with water. Bake meat loaf in pre-heated oven about one hour at 355°F (180°C).

Bavarian Pork Roast

Bavaria

If a plebiscite were to be conducted in Bavaria to ascertain the most popular meat recipe – the winner could be announced in advance: the pork roast. Although this roast from a juicy piece of pork is appreciated in other countries, too, the Bavarian version has surpassed them all. One of the important details is to leave on the thick skin, to cut it criss-cross to get a deliciously crisp rind. A true Bavarian swears: "There is nothing like a pork roast – except two pork roasts!"

2 1/2 lbs. pork (shoulder, rib shoulder) including skin
salt, whole cloves
1 large onion, diced
1 bay leaf
soup greens, chopped
5 peppercorns
1 clove garlic, in halves
1 tsp. cornstarch, ground pepper

Rub salt into meat and place, skin down, onto roasting pan in oven. Pour 1 1/2 cups water over it and roast at 435°F (225°C). After 15 minutes turn meat upside down and cut criss-cross pattern into skin. Stick whole cloves into each intersection and keep roasting for another 45 minutes while basting frequently. Add onion, bay leaf, greens, peppercorns and garlic. Roast another 10 minutes while frequently basting rind with salt water to obtain crispness. Remove meat and keep warm. Bind stock with starch, season to taste with pepper and salt. To keep everything Bavarian style serve with dumplings, salad and a mug of beer.

Beef Roulades

Swabia

"It is as if I had no more wits than any son of Christ or any ordinary person. But I am a big beef eater and believe it is hurting my wits". Modern nutritional scientists would surely contradict William Shakespeare who had expressed this opinion of himself. On the contrary, roulades probably stimulate thought and wit, and, although they are known in many countries, they are rarely more appreciated than in Swabia.

4–6 roulade-size slices (1 3/4 lbs. round beef)
salt, pepper
2–3 onions, diced
1 tbsp. parsley, finely chopped
1 tbsp. butter
4 oz. smoked bacon, diced
2 oz. fillet of anchovies, rinsed
For frying: *3 tbsp. butter*
For gravy: *1–2 tsp. flour, bouillon*

Rub meat slices with salt and pepper. Sauté onion and parsley in butter, spread on meat slices and top with diced bacon and anchovies. Roll up slices, secure with thread and sear in butter all around. Sauté flour in bouillon, add water, cover and simmer till done. Remove thread, pour seasoned gravy over roulades.
Or season meat slices, brush on mustard, add raw onions, bacon and slivers of gherkins, roll up, secure and sear. Toward end, add 5 fl.oz. of sour cream, quickly boil gravy and strain.

Black Forest
Cherry Cake

Baden

A Persian Eunuch is said to have invented this cake while he was chef at the harem in order to round out the figures of the calif's ladies. Whether this is right or wrong, Black Forest Cherry Cake is only cherry cake if it tastes like it. To use essence of cherry, for example, would be a mortal sin.

3 1/2 oz. of sour (morello) cherry preserves
1 prepackaged cake bottom layer (torte shell)
2 thin chocolate cake layers (bake from chocolate cake mix)*
1/2 cup of cherry juice (from cherry jar below)
6 tbsp. sugar
2 tbsp. unbleached flour
1/2 lb. morello cherries from glass jar
1 pinch each cinnamon, ground cloves
3 cups rich cream
4 tbsp. sugar
1 good sized shot glass of Kirschwasser (cherry brandy)
1 tbsp. Knox unflavored gelatin
chocolate shavings for decoration

Spread the cherry preserves on top of bottom layer and put one chocolate cake layer on top. Boil about half the cherry juice with 6 tbsp. sugar. Mix the flour with the remaining cold cherry juice. Add the cherries and spices and allow to cool. Now place the cherry mixture on top of cake. Prepare whipped cream, adding 4 tbsp. sugar and Kirschwasser. Separately dissolve gelatin in 4 tbsp. cold water, let stand 10 minutes, then heat while stirring (do not boil) until liquid is clear. Allow to cool to room temperature and fold in whipped cream.
Spread half of this mixture on top of cake, add the second chocolate cake layer and cover entire cake with remaining whipped cream. After it has stiffened, sprinkle chocolate shavings on top.

* Note: In Germany chocolate cake layers can be bought off the shelf.

Black Forest Cherry Casserole

Baden

The Roman field marshal Licinius Lucullus was not only an outstanding general but also a gregarious gourmet and a friend of the convivial life style. From one of his victorious campaigns in Asia Minor he brought the cherry home to Italy after the destruction of the town of Cerasus. He had it grown in hundreds of plantations until it was also transplanted across the Alps into the Upper Rhine Valley. Its Latin name, Prunus cerasus, still reminds of the conquered town. What a triumphant advance this booty has made!

4 tbsp. sugar
4 oz. pitted (morello) cherries
1 shot glass cherry brandy (Kirschwasser)
4 tbsp. butter
5 tbsp. flour
1 1/4 cups milk
3 egg yolks
3 egg whites
some butter and sugar

First, mix 1 tbsp. of sugar with the pitted cherries and the cherry brandy and allow to stand. Melt butter in a small pan and add the flour to it. Mix thoroughly and set aside. In another pan boil the milk and add 3 tbsp. sugar. After a short cooling period combine it with the flour/butter mixture until it starts to stiffen. Add the egg yolks and mix well. Beat egg whites until stiff and gently fold into the dough together with the cherries. Pour the finished mixture into a medium-sized buttered and sugared casserole. Bake in pre-heated 360°F (180°C) oven for approx. 25 minutes.

Black Forest Medaillons of Venison

Baden

Medaillons of venison, sliced fillet pieces shaped like medals or coins, belong to the aristocratic repertoire of virtually all recognized great chefs. To be served with hand-made Spätzle is in the old Baden tradition and also a nod in the direction of neighboring Swabia. A shot of Black Forest Kirschwasser, ameliorated by red wine, add the sweet-tart taste of native cranberries, and the magic of the entire taste spectrum an enchanting land of wine and forests can offer will unfold on your tongue.

*1 1/2–1 3/4 lbs. venison of deer medaillons
or one piece of leg of deer, same weight
salt, pepper, some butter
approx. 10–12 oz. of (morello) cherries, fresh or
frozen
5 fl.oz. red wine
1 tsp. cornstarch
1 tbsp. cranberries
5 fl.oz. rich cream
2 tbsp. Kirschwasser (cherry brandy)*

Season medaillons with salt and pepper. Braise for two minutes on each side in hot butter. Put aside but keep warm. Pit the cherries and bring to boil in red wine. Thicken with cornstarch and purée, together with the cranberries, in blender at highest speed setting. Pass the purée through a fine sieve and gently blend in the cream by hand and add Kirschwasser to taste. Place the braised meat on platter and pour the sauce on top. Serve with Spätzle (see Spätzle recipe, page 184). A dry Pinot Noir or rosé is recommended.

Blushing Virgin

Lower Saxony

No one knows how this dessert ever obtained its name, however, while it melts on your tongue there is no limit to letting your phantasy roam and dream up all sorts of romantic connotations. Well cooled and served with vanilla sauce or cream this "sweet girl" is definitely going to be a delight.

1 quart buttermilk
3 oz. package of red Jell-O gelatin dessert
(choose your favorite flavor)
1 package vanilla flavored sugar or 1 tsp. vanilla
extract
4 tbsp. sugar

Add 2 cups boiling buttermilk to gelatin. Stir until dissolved about 2 minutes. Add 2 cups cold buttermilk. Pour into large dessert bowl or small individual bowls and chill until set. Serve with vanilla sauce or cream.

Bread Dumplings

Bavaria

Bavarian dumplings are supposed to have helped win a war. According to legend the Lower Bavarian town of Deggendorf one time was under siege by a Bohemian tribe called the Hussites. But the Deggendorfers were soon out of ammunition. They didn't give up easily, however, and were shooting at the enemy with stale, hard dumplings. The make-shift ammunition turned out to be a miracle weapon because the Hussites withdrew, perhaps because they had only known long, oblong-shaped dumplings at home and must have taken the Bavarian national dish for real cannon balls.

10–12 stale rolls, salt
1 1/2 cups of warm milk
1 tbsp. butter
1 tsp. onions, chopped
1/2 tsp. parsley, finely minced
3–4 eggs
salt water

Cut rolls in thin slices, place in bowl, salt, add milk, cover and allow to soak 30 minutes. Sauté onions and parsley, add to the soaked slices together with eggs. Knead everything thoroughly. With moistened hands form a small test dumpling and drop into boiling salt water. If it doesn't flake or fall apart, form about 6–8 dumplings and put in salt water. Cover and allow water to boil again. Uncover partially and simmer for 20 minutes. Dumplings are to Bavarians what Spätzle are to the Swabians – their national side dish.

Camembert
Cheese Spread

Bavaria

About 200 years ago the Norman peasant woman Marie Harel discovered a soft cheese which has been imitated around the world – Camembert. The Bavarians have gone the French one better by using this fine French invention and adding a double-cream cheese to a mixture, which, after adding spices becomes the Bavarian "Obatzda", dialect for "angepatzter" or cheese mixture.

1 lb. very mature Camembert
1/2 lb. Philadelphia Cream Cheese
6 tbsp. butter
salt, pepper, caraway seeds, paprika
2 medium-size onions, chopped
5 tbsp. beer

In bowl squash and mix Camembert and Philadelphia Cream Cheese with fork and mix thoroughly. Blend in butter and other ingredients. Add beer toward end and mix again. Serve with radishes, rolls, pretzels – and don't ever forget a large glass of beer!

Casserole of Asparagus

Baden

Once upon a time, a prelate who was well known for raising excellent asparagus had invited a bishop to personally dig an asparagus. And behold, one of them had already stuck its little head out of the soil. The bishop tried to dig it with his knife, the asparagus rose and rose and turned out to be a giant monster. Host and bishop almost cracked up because the prelate had had this risqué specimen specially made and painted by a lathe turner.

2 1/2 lbs. asparagus
Béchamel sauce:
3 tbsp. butter
2 onions, diced
4 tbsp. bacon, diced
3 tbsp. flour
1 1/4 cups asparagus water
1 1/4 cups milk
salt, pepper
1 tbsp. lemon juice
1 tbsp. cream
4 egg yolks, 4 egg whites
4 tbsp. (Black Forest) ham, diced

Pare and boil asparagus till tender. Save water. Place into four 4″ custard cups enough one inch asparagus pieces to serve as bottom layer. Cut 20 asparagus tips long enough to extend about one inch above custard cups and place aside.
Béchamel sauce: Now sauté in butter the cubed onions and bacon, add flour and sauté till light yellow; add the asparagus water and milk, boil and season with salt, pepper, lemon and cream. Purée the remaining asparagus and fold in the egg yolks and whipped egg whites. Vertically place 5 asparagus tips around the edge of the custard cups. Pour the purée to top of cups and place in oven at medium heat. Sprinkle chopped ham on top prior to serving.

Chervil Soup

Palatinate

The classical food to be eaten on the day before Good Friday in predominantly Catholic Palatinate – and not only there – is chervil soup. Its distinctly tart taste is appreciated by gourmets while it also starts people to get in the right mood for the Good Friday Passion. On a more mundane level, many health-oriented individuals have re-discovered chervil as a health food in the last few years.

3 oz. ground unripe spelt grain (if not available, flour)
3 1/2 tbsp. butter
1 1/2 quarts bouillon
pepper, salt
1 pinch of nutmeg
2 hands full fresh chervil, finely chopped
1 cup cream
roasted bread crumbs, as a condiment

Sauté ground spelt in butter golden brown. Add bouillon, season with pepper, salt, nutmeg and boil 15 minutes. Add fresh chervil. Bring to quick boil. When boiling stops add cream and serve together with the bread crumbs.

Chicken in Wine Sauce

Palatinate

There is always a suspicion that surely this recipe must have been plagiarized from neighbouring Alsace since coq-au-vin is such an internationally recognized recipe. Without trying to diminish the culinary achievements of the famous French or Alsation chefs, there is also the likelihood that someone in a wine-rich area such as the Palatinate certainly must have tried to cook a juicy chicken in wine. A Riesling, Silvaner or Müller-Thurgau, in short, a dry white wine is most suitable. And noodles will taste a lot better than rice.

2 fresh chickens
salt, pepper
butter for sautéeing
1/2 lb. mushrooms, sliced
1 glass pickled cocktail onions
1 1/4 cups white wine
1 1/4 cups cream
flour, if desired

Quarter chickens, rub with salt and pepper and in skillet sauté well. Add mushrooms and cocktail onions (without liquid) and sauté. Add wine and simmer for 30 minutes, covered. Remove chickens, keep warm. Loosen stock from bottom of skillet, add cream and thicken a little, if you desire, with very little flour. Season well with wine, salt and pepper. Pour sauce over chickens in a serving dish.

Chicken Paté

Rhineland
(8–10 Persons)

To prevent your chickens' eggs from winding up in someone else's nests you will have to scatter their feed in a circle on Easter Day, says an old tale. But to prevent your chickens from winding up in the oven would be to forego the pleasures of this paté.

2 small chickens, salt water
1 onion, sliced
1 bay leaf
6 juniper berries
18 oz. chicken liver
3 1/4 cups white wine
1 onion
2 tbsp. unflavored Knox gelatin
1 1/4 cups chicken broth
salt, pepper and curry to taste
1 tbsp. soy sauce
10 pepper corns
1 whole clove
soup greens
2 tbsp. whipped cream

Night before: Boil chickens in salt water with sliced onion and spices for 50–60 minutes. During last 15 minutes add liver. Strain and put liver in refrigerator. Bone chickens and soak meat (abt. 1 ¼ lbs.) in wine overnight.

Following day: Strain wine. Put chicken meat, liver and onion through meat grinder. Stir gelatin in 8 tbsp. cold water. Let stand 10 minutes and add to warm (not boiling) chicken broth, stirring and seasoning well. Mix with ground meat and fold in whipped cream. Pour mixture into rectangular paté form and cool several hours. If you want to serve paté on a platter, pour a few layers of gelatin in form first and put down some decorations.

Coburg
Potato Dumplings

Frankonia

Coburg, in Upper Frankonia, is widely acclaimed for the remnants of medieval architecture and the magnificient Renaissance buildings it harbors within its walls. The "Veste", a fortress situated high above the town, is proudly referred to as the "Crown of Frankonia". Among many other artifacts it also houses a priceless collection of graphic art from world-famous artists, Dürer and Cranach included among the more than 300.000 drawings. This immense collection bears witness to the strong artistic dedication of the ruling princes, of which the Sachsen-Coburg-Gotha line undoubtedly was the most renowned. But this enlightened attitude was not only limited to the fine arts. It also encompassed the culinary arts within that liberal attitude toward a sophisticated lifestyle.

4 1/2 lbs. potatoes
2 quarts salt water
1 large pinch of salt
2 stale rolls or dry bread
3 tbsp. butter or shortening

Pare raw potatoes, slice half the amount and boil in salt water. Press soft potatoes through masher or sieve, stir until smooth and keep warm while setting aside. Grate remaining half of raw potatoes into the salt water and pass everything through a cheesecloth over a bowl. Squeeze out thoroughly. Save the starch collecting at bottom of bowl and combine mashed potatoes, raw potatoes and starch. Knead thoroughly and salt to taste. Cut rolls or dry bred in to 1/4" croutons and roast in skillet in hot fat. Form dumplings and place croutons in center. Boil in covered salt water for 30 minutes. Serve immediately.

Cod in White Wine

Hesse

Cod has always been one of the favorites among German housewives. It used to be rather inexpensive and provided an ample supply of proteins and other essential elements. Although its price today almost equals that of meat, it is still sold in substantial quantities. It is caught by floating "fish factories" in fishing grounds around Greenland, Iceland, the Faroes and along the Norwegian coast. These ships process and deep-freeze the fish directly on board from where it is passed along the "deep-freeze chain" right into the most remote inland households. But even fresh cod is available in every seafood retail store.

1 3/4 lbs. fillet of cod (or haddock)
some vinegar or lemon juice
4 tbsp. margarine
2 tbsp. flour
1 onion, diced
1 1/4 cups dry white wine
salt, pepper, fresh dill
5 fl.oz. cream, beat semi-stiff

Wash fish and rub with vinegar or lemon juice. Cut in bite-size pieces. Melt margarine, add flour and onion, stir while adding wine until onions are sautéed light brown. Season with salt and pepper, add fish. Allow to cook for 15 minutes at medium heat. Toward end add plenty of chopped dill and cream. Serve with boiled potatoes and salad.

Cream of Trout Soup with Fennel

Lower Saxony

Stream trout and fennel – with the smoky taste of bacon makes a very special soup. Served with toast it can be a light meal or an appetizing starter for an enjoyable dinner.

2 stream trout, gutted
1 1/2 quarts water, salt
1 small bunch soup greens
3 juniper berries, crushed
1 bay leaf, 1 onion, sliced
1 piece smoked bacon
2 small fennel plants
lemon juice
1/2 cup wine brandy (e.g. cognac)
salt, white pepper
3 tbsp. butter
1/2 cup flour
grated nutmeg
5 fl.oz. cream

Add trout to lightly salted water together with chopped greens, spices, onion and bacon. Simmer 20 minutes. Remove trout. Dice fennel root (put aside leaves) and add to broth. Allow to cool. Fillet trout and cut into bite-size pieces. Marinate in lemon juice, brandy, salt and pepper. In skillet sauté butter and flour, add strained fish broth, nutmeg and cream. Add pieces of trout and serve. Spread fresh, chopped fennel leaves on soup.

Crème of Wine Cake

Palatinate

You guessed it! Of course, there is a "Torte" worthy of any wine growing area, combining grape and wine. It is the answer to the cherry cake from Baden or Switzerland and it is so incredibly tempting that you won't stop with just one piece once you have started. You can't even feel it sliding down for all its smoothness. Take heart, the next diet will begin on Monday!

For the dough:
1 2/3 cups flour
7 oz. butter
2 egg yolks
4 1/2 tbsp. sugar
2 tbsp. wine brandy (cognac is just fine)

For the filling:
2 egg yolks
5 tbsp. sugar
5 fl.oz. white wine, not too dry
1 1/2 tbsp. Knox unflavored gelatin
2 egg whites
1 1/4 cups rich cream
1/2 lb. white grapes
1 tbsp. apricot jam
1 1/2 oz. sliced almonds
1 tbsp. butter

Mix and knead ingredients for dough. Grease springform and cover bottom and sides with dough. Put in refrigerator for 20 minutes. Bake in oven abt. 20 minutes at medium heat. Allow to cool.

Filling: In bowl beat egg yolks and 2 tbsp. water until foamy. Stir in sugar and wine. In small saucepan stir gelatin in 4 tbsp. cold water until smooth, let stand 10 minutes then heat (do not boil) until liquid is clear. Allow to cool some and stir into mixture. Beat egg whites and cream until stiff, fold into solidifying crème mixture. Pour crème into pie crust and decorate with pitted half-grapes. Chill. Remove from springform and spread jam around edge. Roast almond slices in butter and stick on jam.

Düsseldorf
Veal Cutlets

Rhineland

Looking up recipes in old cookbooks we find that meat dishes were primarily prepared in kitchens of the affluent middle classes. "Only the very prosperous freeholder eats meat on a Sundaye, rarely on week dayes, verily no more than twenty times as a year is longe", quotes a chronicle from 1803. Since the income from selling cattle was very important to the landholder, the farming girl who had fed a fattened calf would usually receive a "feeding money" for her devotion – usually one Mark.

4 veal cutlets
1 egg yolk
1/2 lb. lean bacon, diced
1 cup mushrooms, diced
2 onions, finely chopped
1 tbsp. parsley, chopped
1/2 tsp. salt
1 pinch pepper
1 egg
3 tbsp. dried bread crumbs
shortening

Bone cutlets and put through meat grinder. Scrape bones clean. Cut off end of bone. Combine egg yolk, bacon, mushrooms, onions, parsley and ground meat and mix thoroughly. Season with salt and pepper. Shape meat mixture to four cutlets and stick piece of bone in each. Put each in beaten egg and bread crumbs on both sides, fry golden brown in hot fat. Serve with carrots and beans and a Rhine or Moselle wine.

East Frisian Bean Stew

Frisia

Stews are enjoying a growing popularity these days – they are no longer considered a "pauper's meal" and can be most appetizing if prepared with imagination and given a piquant note.

In some parts of East Frisia they may even serve pickled herring and apple sauce with this stew. That may not be to everyone's taste, however, it wouldn't hurt to try just once.

2 1/4 lbs. sliced green beans
3/4 lb. lean bacon or pork cutlets, pickled
3 tbsp. butter
1 1/4 lbs. potatoes, large cubes
2 1/2 cups water
1 pinch salt
nutmeg to taste

Put all ingredients into large covered pot and stew for a good hour. Remove bacon or cutlets, arrange on platter. Keep warm. Mash beans and potatoes to your liking and serve in bowl. A tasty beer will round off this hearty meal.

East Frisian Butter Cake

Frisia

The great Roman historian Plinius the Elder reported in his "Naturalis Historia" of certain barbaric peoples – he included the Frisians foremost among them – who were "even using butter" as an ingredient in their meals. We cannot be certain as to whether he knew this cake or he might have changed his mind. Custom in Frisia has it that this cake is also served at wakes together with the famous East Frisian tea. So there, Mr. Plinius the Elder!

1 1/2 oz. compressed yeast or 3 tbsp. dry active yeast
1 1/4 lbs. flour
1 1/4 cups milk
4 tbsp. sugar
1 pinch salt
1 egg
For frosting:
5 oz. butter
5 oz. sugar (in graduated cup measure)
1–2 tsp. cinnamon

Mix yeast with abt. one quarter of the flour, some lukewarm milk and a pinch of sugar, cover and set aside for abt. 15 minutes in warm place. Add remaining milk, sugar, salt, flour and egg, knead well. Roll out dough on bread board, place on cookie sheet and pierce it several times with fork.
Frosting: Now mix butter with sugar, add cinnamon to taste and spread frosting evenly on dough. Bake 20 minutes in pre-heated oven at 390°F (200°C). Tastes best if served fresh.

Eckenheim
Herb Veal Roast

Hesse

A Frankfurt citizen at the beginning of the 19th century wrote: "Frankfurt's cuisine is equal to that of Vienna and Hamburg, it even surpasses them through a touch of French influence, German suckling piglet and collared pork. It holds the middle line between French over-sophistication and British-Nordic coarseness, a wise balance between the meat pots of Egypt, piquant sauces and ragouts and heavy Germanic farinaceous foods". The Eckenheim Herb Veal Roast nicely represents that wise balance.

2 1/2 lbs. breast of veal without bone
salt, pepper
one bunch each of chives, parsley, chervil, tarragon, basil, dill
2 onions
1/2 cup dried bread crumbs
2 eggs
1 1/4 cups water
2 tbsp. oil
3–4 tbsp. butter
1 1/4–2 1/2 cups bouillon
1 tbsp. cornstarch
5 fl.oz. cream

Wash meat and dry. Rub in salt and pepper from both sides. Finely chop all herbs and onions and combine with bread crumbs, eggs and water. Mix homogeneously, season with salt and pepper and spread evenly on the "inside" side of the meat but leave a one inch border all around. Carefully roll up lengthwise and secure with twine. Brush with oil. Heat butter in roasting pan and roast meat in 435°F (225°C) oven for abt. 90 minutes. Add bouillon occasionally. Remove meat from pan. Keep warm while adding starch and cream, in that order, to broth. Season to taste.

Eel on Fresh Sage

Hesse

This eel recipe owes its flavor to the slightly bitter tasting sage, a typically Mediterranean spice. Even the ancient Romans knew how to appreciate the seasoning effects of the spice and the Italians of today can perform culinary wonders with it. One has to differentiate between the so-called genuine sage and the muscatel sage, the latter having a rather pronounced lavender aroma.
If at all possible, try to use fresh, genuine sage leaves – they will reward your culinary labors with their delicate flavor.

1 fresh river eel (approx. 2 to 2 1/2 lbs.)
salt
fresh, genuine sage leaves
1/4 lb. butter

Rub the gutted eel with salt and then wash it. Dry with paper towels. Wrap sage leaves around eel with the aid of thread. Tie head and tail together and fry in butter on both sides. Nice brick oven bread and butter, a shot of clear brandy (aquavit type) and a cool beer will make you feel as if you were at the Ritz.

Egg Nog à la Frisia

Frisia

The capital city of rum is also Germany's northern-most town. This honor was not only bestowed upon Flensburg because of her industrious merchants but, above all, because of her pure and soft water. The imported Jamaican rum which is normally highly concentrated is usually refined down to a potable 50% alcohol content and even that concentration is known to knock many a seasoned sailor flat on his buttocks.

Per Person:
1 egg yolk
1–2 tbsp. confectioner's sugar
1 cup hot rum
hot water to taste

Beat egg yolk and sugar until foamy. Add rum, heat in double boiler. Fill into rum glasses and dilute with hot water to taste. Dilution is not mandatory!

Elderberry "Champagne"

Lower Saxony

If you bring along a bottle of your home-made elderberry champagne to a dinner party as a gift for the hostess, you will not only be the envy of the other guests but you can be sure to be re-invited.

abt. 20–30 elderberry fruit clusters
7 quarts of water
2 1/4 lbs. sugar
peel from 2 lemons
2 oz. tartaric acid

Put all ingredients in crock, stir well and leave for 72 hours, covered. Strain through cheesecloth, bottle and cork loosely. Place in sunshine two to four days until liquid begins to bubble. Place in your cellar or other cool place till next spring. Prosit!

Filled Eggs
à la Cologne

Rhineland

You can prepare these eggs as a warm hors d'œuvre or as a small snack in-between. But if you need something after celebrating all night against that hangover feeling the morning after, why not try a Roman variation: take olive oil instead of melted butter and anchovy paste instead of the spices. You will be going back two thousand years using a Mr. Apicius' antidote. He knew what he was talking about being a gourmet and no slouch himself!

4 hard-boiled eggs
2 1/2 tbsp. butter
1 tbsp. parsley, finely chopped
4 raw eggs
5 fl.oz. white wine
1 tsp. salt
1 pinch pepper
1/2 tsp. nutmeg
4 slices of toast
5 fl.oz. white wine
1 tomato
parsley for garnishing

Halve hard-boiled eggs, remove yolks and squash thoroughly with a fork. In skillet melt butter and first work in yolks, then add parsley and raw eggs. Mix well. Slowly add wine while stirring. Season with salt, pepper, nutmeg and stir long enough until right consistency has been obtained. Fill egg halves, put slices of toast on pre-heated platter and arrange filled egg halves on them. Dilute remaining portion of egg yolk mixture with wine, bring to boil several times and pour over filled eggs. Garnish with small slices of tomato and whole parsley.

Fillet of Fish with Herbs

Palatinate

Unlike some other German provinces the Palatinate cannot call any large lakes its own. Nevertheless, there has never been a lack of fish because all the rivers and streams of the region, as tributaries of the Rhine river, were teeming with trout and other fish. So much so that little rascals could catch them with their bare hands. The Rhine and the network of its old river beds supplied pike, eel, tench and river salmon, as highly priced as they were highly prized. Today, these fish have virtually become extinct due to industrial contamination of the Rhine. Therefore, we have based this recipe on North Sea fish such as cod or haddock. The meal will taste just as deliciously, however.

3 lbs. fillet of cod or haddock
salt, pepper, juice from 1 lemon
1 1/4 cups dry white wine
2 tbsp. butter
5 carrots
1/2 bunch of celery
3 stalks leek } *cut in slivers*
3 medium sized onions, finely chopped
1 cup cream
1/2 lb. smoked bacon, cut in strips
1 bunch parsley, finely chopped

Wash and dry fillet, place in flat casserole dish. Rub with salt, pepper and lemon juice. Add wine to cover. Allow to steep 1 to 2 hours. Sauté carrots, celery, leek and onions and spread over fish, pour cream over it. Top with bacon strips in a criss-cross pattern. Place in pre-heated oven at medium heat for 45 minutes. Spread parsley on top and serve with a cool, dry white wine.

Fillet of Pork

Swabia

A nicely prepared fillet of pork is a culinary pleasure in itself, as any gourmet knows. But this delicacy can be further refined by adding scallions. The "little onions" are not related to the onion family but are a relative of chives, named after the french "échalotte". The knights brought them back to Europe from Palestine and Asia Minor from their crusades. Scallions soon found favor all over Europe.

Approx. 1 3/4 lbs. fillet of pork
2 slices smoked bacon
2 scallions, finely chopped
3–4 tbsp. shortening
6 oz. fresh mushrooms, sliced
mustard, ketchup
one pinch of pepper and salt, each
bottled (pork) gravy as desired
1 tbsp. sour cream

Cut fillet in narrow slices and bacon to slivers. Sauté bacon slivers until transparent, add scallions and place fillets on top. Fry quickly at high heat on both sides until golden brown. Skim off some of the fat, add mushrooms, mustard, ketchup and season to taste. Toward end add some gravy to taste and sour cream. Serve with Spätzle (recipe see page 184) and fresh salad.

Fillet of Pork
on Potato Pancakes

Lower Saxony

Even though potato pancakes cause more work than simple boiled potatoes or frozen potato pancakes from the supermarket, we feel they taste so much better that it is worth the labor. Your eyes and palate will gratefully acknowledge it.

2 fillets of pork (1 3/4–2 lbs.)
salt, white pepper
4 tbsp. mustard
some flour, oil
3 scallions, chopped
1/2 cup white wine
1 cup crème fraîche or sour cream

Rub fillets with salt, pepper and one tbsp. mustard. Roll in flour and in skillet sauté in hot oil. Place in oven for 15 minutes at 390°F (200°C). Meanwhile prepare your potato pancakes (recipe see page 136). Remove meat from oven and pan, set aside but keep warm. Add scallions and remaining mustard to broth, stir while adding wine and cream. Cut fillets in individual portions and arrange on pancakes. Add gravy. A salad from spinach leaves with vinegar and oil dressing is a lovely condiment.

Fillet of Trout on Cream of Sorrel Sauce

Baden
(for one person)

We know that the almost extinct, speckled Black Forest wildwater trout has achieved international renown. That's why you will find so many high-browed expressions in this recipe. In comparison, the word "sorrel" almost sounds pedestrian but it does add the crowning touch to this delicate dish.

1 trout (any trout)
salt, pepper, nutmeg, some butter
Cream of sorrel sauce:
2 scallions, finely chopped
1 shot glass of dry, white wine
4 tbsp. Fumet de poisson (canned fish concentrate)
2 liqueur glasses of Vermouth
8 tbsp. of sour cream or crème fraîche
salt, ground pepper
1 oz. of sorrel
1 1/2 tbsp. of butter

Clean trout inside and out under running water, dry and fillet, remove skin. Season fillets with salt, pepper and a little nutmeg. Sauté in butter, use medium heat. Serve right away on top of cream of sorrel sauce.

Cream of sorrel sauce: Cook and sharply reduce scallions, white wine, Fumet de poisson and Vermouth. Add sour cream and quickly reduce again, add salt and freshly ground pepper and strain. Wash the sorrel as plucked, cut in narrow strips and add to the still hot sauce (don't boil) together with 1 1/2 tbsp. butter. Stir smoothly. This last phase must be quite short. A dry white or chilled rosé wine will complement this delicacy.

Frankfurter Kranz

Hesse

Some things cannot and should not be translated because it would only diminish the original meaning or fame. Let's just say this is a sort of short cake with a long history. Goethe, a Frankfurt citizen and poet laureate, must have been left speechless on this tasty cake that he never even so much as mentioned it. Need any more proof? Then try it!

Dough:
1/4 lb. + 1 tbsp. butter
4 egg yolks
5 oz. sugar (measured in graduated cup)
grated peel of 1/2 lemon
1 1/4 cups flour
3/4 cup cornstarch
2 tsp. baking powder
4 egg whites
Butter crème:
2 cups milk (or follow instructions on pudding)
1/2 cup sugar
1 package of vanilla pudding (3 1/2 oz.)
9 oz. butter
3/4 cup confectioner's sugar
2 tbsp. rum
croquant for frosting (a mixture of roasted almonds and caramalized sugar)

Stir soft butter until smooth. Keep stirring and alternately add egg yolks and a few tbsp. sugar until you have smooth yellow paste. Separately mix lemon peel, flour, starch and baking powder and add one tbsp. at a time to dough, while stirring. Finally, beat egg whites stiff and fold into dough carefully. Pour into greased 8″ springform pan with tube inset and bake 30 minutes at medium heat. Allow to cool. For **butter crème,** cook pudding from milk, sugar and pudding powder. Stir frequently while it cools to prevent skin. Stir soft butter and confectioner's sugar until foamy and combine with room temperature pudding, a spoon at a time. Finally, add rum for refinement. Cut cake in two, horizontally, fill with crème in center, replace top half and spread crème on all sides. Cover with croquant all around.

Frankonian Pork Roast

Frankonia

Pork still ranks among the favorite meats of the German Hausfrau and rightly so since a whole new breed of very lean porkers has been bred in the postwar years. Almost every region has its own recipes and almost every housewife has her own slight variation. It would simply be impossible to attempt to list the innumerable possibilities. You must try this recipe with potato dumplings (recipe see page 42) and cole slaw.

2 1/2 lbs. pork loin roast (center cut roast only)
one pinch each of salt, caraway seed and mar-
joram
1 bunch parsley, finely chopped
3/4 cup water
1 large onion
1 slice rye bread
1/2 glass of white wine

Bone the meat and rub with spices and chopped parsley. Place on rack in oven. Put in shallow oven pan underneath rack the chopped bones, water, onion and rye bread. Cook with medium heat about 90 minutes while basting frequently. Strain the broth and season with white wine.

Frankonian
Veal Sweetbreads

Frankonia

Sweetbreads is the culinary term for the thymus gland of calves or lambs. It is located in the front part of the chest cavity. It weighs between 1/2 lb. to 3/4 lb. and regulates the growth and formation of bones in the young animal. The appetizingly white sweetbreads are considered a delicacy because of their tenderness and their delicate taste. But taste has its price – even at the butcher shop. Always buy them fresh or frozen as they will not keep as long as other meats.

2–3 sweetbreads
vinegar and water mixture
1 pinch of salt and pepper, each
1/2 bunch of parsley, finely chopped
6–7 tbsp. butter

Rinse sweetbreads in water frequently until blood stops oozing out. Remove cartilage, place in strainer and pour boiling vinegar-water mixture over them. This will retain the white appearance and loosen the skin. After skinning slice cross-wise and season with salt, pepper and chopped parsley. In skillet fry in hot butter until golden yellow and serve immediately with the butter from skillet. Serve with boiled or home fried potatoes, fresh vegetables or salad.

Fried North Sea Sole (Butt)

Frisia

The problem with the animal kingdom of the deep is nomenclature. Unless you take the Latin name for each species, you will end up with a confusing selection of names depending on where and who you ask. Our fish is called a plaice by ichthyologists but it is also a sole, a butt, a flatfish etc. Let's call it sole for our purposes.

Have the fish cleaned out by your fish monger or you can do it yourself. Since it isn't easy to fry sole without having it stick to the bottom of your skillet, here is Grandma's easy solution: wash the fish, dry it on paper towels, pull it through a beaten egg and press it into lightly salted bread crumbs or flour. Sole tastes best in May or June.

4 North Sea Soles
1 egg
1 1/3 cups dried bread crumbs
3 tbsp. salt
shortening or melted fat from 3 oz. of smoked bacon

Scale the fish and clean under running water. Bread as indicated above. Bring fat to high heat and fry fish for 5 minutes on either side until golden brown. Serve with potato salad (recipe see page 138) or with boiled potatoes and melted butter. A fresh salad also goes well with it.

Frisian Mussels

Frisia

Mussels are also called Pfahlmuscheln in German because they love to cling to pilings in the water, offshore. They belong to the most important edible shellfish species native to the European and North American coasts. As long ago as the 13th century, French fishermen noticed that they grew better on wooden pilings than at the bottom of the sea. They started the first mussel breeding grounds. The "poor man's oyster" is raised particularly along the Northern French, the Dutch and the East Frisian seashore.

7 lbs. mussels
1 bunch of greens (leek, celery, carrots, parsley), chopped
3 tbsp. butter
2–3 onions, sliced
10 whole peppercorns
1 pinch of salt
1 large glass of white wine

Wash and brush mussels thoroughly under cold, running water. Boil the greens, melted butter, onion rings, peppercorns, salt and white wine about 10–15 minutes. Add mussels and boil rapidly for 6 minutes. Be sure they are covered with water. Remove mussels and serve with brick oven dark bread and butter.
Note: If one or the other mussel shell should remain closed after boiling, it is better to discard it, just in case.

Grandma's L'il Old Fillet of Herring

Westphalia

Herring once was the most important fish on our tables. So much so that the City of Hamburg passed an ordinance around the turn of the century forbidding housewives to feed herring more than twice a week. Today, herring has become very rare through overfishing and is (therefore?) considered a delicacy. You can replace part of the sour cream with yoghurt if you want to watch your waistline.

4 pickled herring
For marinade:
1 1/4 cups water
2 tbsp. vinegar
1/2 bay leaf
1/2 tsp. whole pepper corns
1/2 tsp. juniper berries;
2 tsp. sugar
2 onions, thinly sliced
2 tart apples, cored, skinned and coarsely grated or slivered
1–2 gherkins, thinly sliced
1 1/2 cups sour cream

Soak gutted herring in cold water overnight. Skin and fillet, beginning along "spine". For **marinade,** boil water, vinegar, spices and sugar quickly. Allow to cool and steep herring in it 3–4 hours. Remove fillets from marinade, dab dry and place on platter and evenly spread onion rings, apple slivers and gherkin slices on top. Dilute sour cream with 1–2 tbsp. marinade and pour over herring. Cool platter in refrigerator before serving with boiled potatoes or hearty brick oven bread.

Halibut
à la Westerland

Frisia

There has always been a sort of natural and quiet congeniality among the citizens of the Hanseatic League, the North Frisians, the East Frisians and the people of the open lowlands of the Netherlands. Many a Flemish expression has been absorbed into the Frisian vocabulary as time went by or vice versa, for Frisians they are all. One of the words is "sutje". It means as much as "slowly", "gently" but also "exactly on the minute". There is nothing worse than a wishy-washy fish or one that has been cooked too long. So, better keep a close look at the clock – your palate will appreciate it.

1 halibut of abt. 2–2 1/2 lbs.
3 3/4 cups water
3 tbsp. salt
2 tbsp. butter
3 tbsp. flour
1 1/4 cups fish broth
2 tbsp. butter for sautéeing mushrooms
2 cups mushrooms, sliced
2/3 cup dried bread crumbs
2 tbsp. butter

Clean halibut and boil slowly 15 minutes in salt water. Remove bones and dark skin, cut fish into equal pieces and place in heat-resistant pan, one overlapping the other. Melt 2 tbsp. butter in saucepan, stir in flour and add 1 1/4 cups of the fish broth. Meanwhile sauté mushrooms in butter, add to broth and pour everything over fish in pan. Top with bread crumbs and place butter flakes evenly on top. Cook in 430°F (220°C) oven on low rack for 15 minutes.

Henrietta's Bridal Cake

Westphalia

In her original recipe, the famous Westphalian cookbook author Henriette Davidis suggests garnishing the frosting with myrtle and flower blossoms. This recipe is particulary practical since the cake can be prepared a few days before the big occasion – it will only improve that way.

For the dough:
18 oz. butter
2 1/3 cups granulated sugar
grated peel of 1 lemon
1 tsp. powdered mace (or pinch nutmeg)
12 eggs (separate into yolks and whites)
5 cups grated almonds
4 cups flour
For filling:
4 oz. butter
1 1/4 cups confectioner's sugar
grated peel of 1 lemon
4 egg yolks
juice from 4 lemons
For frosting:
1 1/4 cups confectioner's sugar
juice from 1 lemon

Stir butter in warm bowl until creamy. Slowly add sugar, spices, egg yolks and almonds, toward end add flour and fold in stiffly beaten egg whites. Separate dough into 4 equal portions and bake a flat "bottom" from each in greased springform, 15 minutes at 395°F (200°C), remove and allow to cool. **For filling,** melt butter at low heat, add sugar, lemon peel, egg yolks, lemon juice and mix thoroughly until mixture starts to thicken. Spread filling on three of the baked "bottoms" (not on the top one) and stack them. Allow to cool overnight in refrigerator. With a sharp knife cut around edge of cake for straight edge. **For frosting,** mix confectioner's sugar and lemon juice, brush on top and side and allow to dry.

Hilda Cookies

Rhineland
(approx. 50 pieces)

These cookies exude so much the warmth of Christmas when arranged with love and taste on a nice Yuletide platter. They were named after an aunt who passed her culinary artistry to many of her nieces. Hilda cookies taste best when they are about two weeks old and have softened up a bit. It is best to keep them in a decorative tin box in a cool and safe place. Some members of the family might otherwise be caught with their hands in the cookie jar.

2 1/2 cups flour
6 oz. butter, flaked, cold
2/3 cup sugar
1 egg
2 tbsp. red jelly or good red jam
1 tbsp. confectioner's sugar

Place flour, cold butter flakes, sugar and egg on bread board and cut in butter until dough is forming. Then start kneading with your hands until dough is smooth. Put in refrigerator abt. one hour. Roll out dough rather thinly, cut out round discs about 3″∅. Punch hole in half of discs with a thimble. Put all discs on greased cookie sheet. Bake in pre-heated oven at medium heat abt. 20 minutes. Spread red jelly (currant is ideal) or preferably jam on top of cookies without a hole. Sprinkle cookies with hole with confectioner's sugar and place on top of cookies without a hole. Merry Christmas!

Lamb Roast filled with Savoy Cabbage

Lower Saxony

This recipe originates in the Lüneburg Heather where sheep husbandry used to be the only "industry" for centuries, not unlike the Scottish Highlands.

1 lamb's shoulder (rolled roast) abt. 2–2 1/2 lbs., boned
salt, white pepper
1 head of savoy cabbage
caraway seeds
2 scallions, diced
3 cups fresh mushrooms, sliced
2 tbsp. olive oil, nutmeg
1/2 lb. fresh white bread, crumbled
5 fl.oz. milk
2 egg yolks
1 bunch parsley, chopped
3 tbsp. oil
5 fl.oz. red wine
1 bunch soup greens, chopped
1 stem thyme
2–3 whole pimento corns
3 juniper berries
3 tbsp. crème fraîche or sour cream

Rub meat with salt and pepper. Blanch savoy leaves in boiling water and caraway seeds. Sauté scallions and mushrooms in olive oil, cool and season. Add crumbled bread, milk, egg yolks – stir and heat. Fold in parsley. Place blanched savoy leaves on meat and spread mixture on top. Roll up meat lengthwise, fold in ends and secure. Sear in hot oil all around. Roast in oven 1 hour at 355°F (180°C). Turn meat occasionally. Remove meat, keep warm. Pour off grease and add red wine to broth. Add soup greens and spices. Reduce by one third. Pass gravy through sieve, add crème fraîche or sour cream. Cut meat and serve.

Leathernecks

Lower Saxony

They are called "the big fat beans" in Lower Saxony because that's the way they look when they are cooked. But they also make a hearty meal which can be quite filling and provide plenty of energy quickly. The Navy found out, too, and sailors and leathernecks simply loved them, ready to storm any beachhead – especially if it was strewn with (mer-)maids.

1 lb. white beans (or similar)
8 oz. lean bacon
1 onion
1 lb. carrots, sliced
3 1/4 cups hot bouillon
1 bunch fresh summer savory
salt
white pepper

Night before: Soak beans in plenty of water.
Dice bacon and onion, sauté together until transparent. Add beans and carrots. Add hot bouillon. Put savory on top. Cover and allow to simmer at medium heat for 25 to 30 minutes. Season with salt and pepper.

Leg of Veal

Bavaria

The meat course has always been the center of every meal. That was of even greater importance in the past when eating meat was not considered a matter of course for the average person. One of the more outstanding and popular meat recipes is the "Bavarian State Dinner", the Kalbshaxn, and it can compete with any French specialty. Any Bavarian restaurant deserving its name will list it at the top of their menu.

1 leg of veal
pepper, salt
3 tbsp. butter
1 carrot, sliced
1 onion, halved
1 1/4 cups hot water

Wash the leg of veal, skin it and rub with pepper and salt. Melt butter in roasting pan, add carrot slices, onion and a little water. Put leg of veal in pan and cook in 480°F (250°C) oven for 2 to 2 1/2 hours. Turn the leg frequently and gradually baste with remaining water and broth. For last ten minutes place leg alone on oven rack for browning. Pass broth through sieve and season to taste. Bread dumplings (recipe see page 30) are traditionally served with this gourmet dinner.

Leg of Wild Boar

Rhineland

Hunting game used to be the exclusive privilege of nobility or of the landed gentry, unless, as a 1460 ordinance of the Moselle region put it, "a woman goeth pregnant with childe and she craveth for venison she may despatch her man or servant to seize or catch venison enough to satisfy such craving harmlessley".

1 leg of boar, approx. 2 1/2 lbs., boned
2 shot glasses high-proof juniper brandy (gin)
4 juniper berries, crushed
1/2 tsp. marjoram
1/2 tsp. salt
1 pinch pepper
2 tbsp. clarified butter
2 onions, chopped
5 fl.oz. water
1 1/4 cups red wine
5 fl.oz sour cream
As condiments: 1 lemon, sliced
blackberry jelly or cranberry sauce

Roll up meat and secure with twine. Pour one shot glass of gin over it. Rub meat with crushed juniper berries, marjoram, salt and pepper. Put into roasting pan and pour hot, cleared butter over it and sear at high heat on all sides. Add onions, sauté till golden brown. Add water and wine and roast at moderate heat for abt. 2 1/2 hours. Occasionally turn meat and baste with broth and cold water. Remove meat and keep warm – it should be "rare" inside. Skim fat from broth, strain broth and add sour cream. Season with marjoram, salt and pepper. Before serving, pour other shot glass of gin over roast and light it. Allow to burn – until the alcohol has burnt away. Slice meat and serve with lemon, blackberry jelly or cranberry sauce.

Lentil Soup
and
Frankfurters

Hessia

You absolutely need Frankfurters for this main dish. Frankfurters allegedly were first mentioned in a chronicle at the occasion of the crowning of Emperor Maximilian II in 1562. At that time Frankfurters were only available in winter due to a lack of proper conservation media. Pasteurization in tin cans was only available after 1890 and the delicious sausages started their triumphant voyage around the world. Frankfurters, under German law, may only be made from the best of pork and produced only in a clearly defined area around Frankfurt. Neu-Isenburg at present is the center of the Frankfurter industry.

1 lb. lentils
6 cups bouillon
1 lb. leek, sliced
1/2 lb. carrots, cubed
4 oz. celery stalks, sliced
1/2 lb. lean bacon, diced
2 onions, diced
2 tbsp. vinegar, salt
pepper, fresh ground
8 Frankfurters

Wash lentils. Bring bouillon to boil. Add lentils, leek, carrots and celery. Bring to a quick boil and allow to simmer at low heat about one hour. In skillet fry bacon well, add onions and sauté. Add bacon and onions to soup. Season with vinegar, salt and pepper. Ten minutes before serving add Frankfurters to soup. Never boil Frankfurters. It would ruin their taste and they would burst. Serve with Spätzle (recipe see page 184).

Linen Weaver's Omelet

Westphalia

A poor linen weaver's wife allegedly invented this "stretched" omelet. This omelet is popular throughout Westphalia as a simple but appetizing everyday meal. It is also suitable for using up leftovers. Some other variations use slivered instead of sliced potatoes and add slivers of bacon. At any rate, it is a good, hearty and quick Saturday lunch when the whole family is busy with shopping and other errands.

1 3/4 lbs. boiled potatoes (preferably from day before)
For the batter:
4 eggs
1 1/4 cups flour
1 1/4 cups milk
one pinch each of salt, pepper and nutmeg
2–3 onions, sliced
salt, shortening
1/2 bunch of parsley, chopped

Peel potatoes and slice. Scramble eggs, mix with flour, milk, add salt, pepper and nutmeg. Allow to sit for 20 minutes, stir again.
Fry potatoes and onions in skillet, add salt. Separate into four equal portions and add 1/4 of omelet mix to each portion of potatoes in skillet. Turn carefully, fry on both sides. Put each portion on separate heated plate and sprinkle parsley on top. Serve hot with a nice salad.

Liver Dumplings

Palatinate

Liver dumplings used to be served at least once a week in Palatinate homes. They were called Lewerknepp in dialect. They were also the customary meal on the annual Parish Fair Day. The criterion of good liver dumplings is that they look and taste like liver – and not like bread dumplings.

1 lb. beef liver, finely ground or chopped
3 stale rolls
3 oz. smoked bacon, finely ground or chopped
3 eggs
2 onions
1 bunch parsley, finely chopped
salt, pepper, marjoram, nutmeg
3 tbsp. dried bread crumbs
1 1/2 quarts salt water or bouillon

Soak rolls and squeeze water out with hands and add with bacon and eggs to liver. Sauté onions and parsley and add to mixture together with spices. Mix very thoroughly and put into refrigerator for abt. one hour. Try one or two small dumplings. If they dissolve or flake off, put bread crumbs into mixture. Form dumplings with hands or a spoon and drop into boiling water or bouillon for 15 minutes. Put golden brown fried onion rings on top and serve with Sauerkraut and mashed potatoes.

Liver Dumpling Soup

Bavaria

A really hot soup is good for the stomach and mobilizes the gastric juices for the succeeding courses. Lower Bavaria has a reputation for and appreciation of clear soups garnished with all sorts of dumplings, Spätzle, litte sausages etc. No wonder the liver dumpling soup is one of their favorites. In the old days "liver dumpling soup with small sausages" was served at country weddings. It tastes delightfully and two soup dishes are worth an entire meal.

4 old rolls or abt. 10 dry slices of bread (not toasted)
some salt
1 1/4 cups lukewarm milk
1 tsp. chopped onions
1 tsp. finely chopped parsley
1 heaping tbsp. butter or shortening
a few drops lemon juice
1 pinch marjoram
5–6 oz. of ground liver of beef or veal
2 eggs
6 cups bouillon
chives

Cut rolls in thin slices or cut bread slices into slivers, salt lightly, lightly soak in lukewarm milk and cover. Sauté onions and parsley in heated fat. Add lemon juice, marjoram, ground liver and eggs, mix carefully. Form two or three small test dumplings and drop them into boiling bouillon. Should they be too soft and flake off or dissolve, add bread crumbs, flour or semolina (cream of wheat) to dumpling mixture. Once consistency is right, form four large dumplings and drop into boiling bouillon. Allow to simmer about 20 minutes. The chopped chives are added directly to the soup bowl.

Marinated Beef

Bavaria

This recipe has a historical background and dates back to the numerous French sieges and occupations of Bavaria or Bavarian towns. Although, or perhaps because most martial encounters did not cause much harm, the Bavarians were able to look into French cooking pots and took a liking to the big pieces of beef which the French had soaked in vinegar and red wine and which they called "Bœuf à la mode". That became "Böfflamott" in the Bavarian vernacular – and a culinary hit.

1 1/4 – 1 1/2 lbs. beef (chuck or rib)
Marinade:
3 1/2 cups water, salt
1 – 1 1/4 cups vinegar
1 root of parsley
1 carrot
1 onion
3 peppercorns, 3 pimento corns
2 whole cloves, 2 bay leaves
4 juniper berries
Gravy:
1 tsp. sugar
2 tbsp. shortening
5 tbsp. flour
2 1/2 cups marinade
1 glass (1 1/4 cups) red wine

Put ingredients for **marinade** into pot and bring to boil. Place beef into bowl and pour lukewarm marinade over meat. Cover and steep for two or three days, turning meat in marinade occasionally. Preparing the meal, bring marinade to boil, add water if it is too strong. Put meat into boiling marinade and simmer for 1 1/2 hours. For **gravy,** brown the sugar in hot fat to light yellow, add flour until golden brown and immediately add marinade and red wine, stir and boil slowly for 10 minutes, strain and season to taste. Slice meat and pour gravy over it. Serve with potato dumplings (recipe see page 42) or noodles. A nice salad will round off the meal.

Matjes Herring

Frisia

Matjes herring, in the narrow sense of the term are only the young herring which are caught from the middle of May to early June along the East Coast of Scotland and the Northern Coast of Ireland. Matjes herring should be pickled rather gently. Taste them before using them. If they are too salty for your taste, soak them in water for a few hours.

Fillet of Matjes with Boiled Potatoes

8 fillets of herring
2 onions
1 apple
1 1/4 cups cream
1 pinch sugar and pepper, each
potatoes, depending on demand

Cut onion rings, core and slice apples and arrange with fillets on deep glass dish. Mix cream with sugar and pepper and pour on top.

Fillet Rolls of Matjes on Apple Rings

8 fillets of herring
2 large apples
1 tsp. lemon juice
1 1/4 cups rich cream
1 pinch sugar
1–2 tbsp. horseradish (freshly grated if possible)
1–2 tbsp. cranberries, whole
1 tsp. finely chopped dill

Pare and core apples, cut each into four rings and sprinkle with lemon juice. Beat cream, sugar and horseradish. Place one rolled-up fillet on one apple ring and fill with horseradish sauce. Garnish with cranberries and dill (see photograph).

Serve both recipes with boiled potatoes.

May Wine

Frankonia

Frankonian wine comes in a very odd-shaped bottle called Bocksbeutel, lit. "billy-goat's scrotum". The shape of this short and rather flat bottle has been reserved by law for the wines of Frankonia and the Tauber Valley extending into Baden. The very characteristic taste of Frankonian wines, a fruity, juicy and tart dryness that tingles any palate, originates in the shell-lime soils of the Main River triangle and the Keuper soil of the Steiger Forest. May Wine, on the other hand, obtains its characteristic flavor from fresh woodruff (Waldmeister in German). The recipe is known in other wine-growing areas, even in Berlin, where no wine is grown. Don't leave the woodruff in the wine too long, or it may cause an unpleasant headache. And no sugar, please, for the same reason.

2 bottles white wine (Frankonia)
1 bunch fresh, young woodruff
1 bottle dry champagne

Pour the well-chilled wine into large bowl. Wash woodruff, dab it dry, bind its stems with thread and only allow leaves to dangle in the wine. Remove after 30 minutes and add ice-cold champagne. There is nothing so refreshing!

Munich Royal Regent's Cake

Bavaria

The Royal Regent Luitpold of Bavaria appreciated a cool dip until his old age. He took almost diabolic pleasure in taking a swim in the pool of the Nymphenburg "Badenburg" shortly before dinner. If they liked it or not, his guests had no choice but to join him in this chilly pleasure. Nevertheless, the Royal Regent enjoyed a fine reputation among his subjects as a happy and benign ruler. The Rottenhöfer Pastry Shop, by Royal Appointment, dedicated this cake to Luitpold. °

5 oz. butter
3 egg yolks
3/4 cup sugar
5 fl.oz. milk
1/2 lb. flour
6 tbsp. cornstarch
2 tsp. baking powder
1 pinch salt
3 egg whites
butter for greasing springform
For filling:
4 oz. butter
4 oz. baker's chocolate
2 eggs
1 1/2 tbsp. sugar
5 oz. sweet chocolate for frosting
some butter

Stir butter, egg yolk and sugar till creamy. Add milk, flour, starch, baking powder and salt to get smooth dough. Beat egg whites until stiff and fold into dough. Bake 6–8 layers from dough by spreading 3–4 tbsp. dough on small, greased spring form and bake 8–10 minutes each in 390°F (200°C) oven. Allow to cool. For **filling,** beat butter, the melted chocolate, eggs and sugar until foamy. Spread this mixture on the baked layers alternately but leave top layer free. Heat the sweet chocolate, stir and add some butter. Spread the frosting immediately over entire cake.

Nuremberg Carp

Frankonia

Frankonia is a province of noble residences (Schlösser) and of old, picturesque half-timbered houses. The area between the Jurassic Range and the Frankonian Forest is literally dotted with carp ponds. There are at least five thousand in Upper Frankonia, four thousand in the Upper Palatinate and almost three thousand in the Pegnitz, Regnitz and Wörnitz area. The carps from the Aisch lowlands probably take first prize, followed by the ones from the breeding ponds around Fürth and the quaint town of Hirschau, which are also a first class delicacy.

1 carp (abt. 2–2 1/2 lbs.)
1 bottle of Pilsen beer
salt, pepper, paprika, flour
1 heaping tablespoon clarified butter
2 tbsp. butter
Horseradish sauce:
1/2 cup cream
1 grated apple
1 tbsp. fresh, grated horseradish

Butcher carp, clean and cut in two, lengthwise. Marinade fish halves for abt. 15 minutes in plenty of beer. Then remove halves, rub them with salt, fresh ground pepper and paprika. Roll fish halves in flour and fry in butter in 320°F (160°C) oven, baste occasionally. Carp is ready when gills have turned evenly brown. Drain fat from pan and replace with fresh butter and baste fish with it. Serve immediately with boiled potatoes and parsley.
Horseradish sauce: Beat cream until stiff and carefully fold in grated apple and horseradish.

Nuremberg
Ginger Bread

Frankonia

Nuremberg and its ginger bread – it has probably made this ancient city on the Pegnitz River as famous as her great sons or her long history. Ginger bread, the pre-holiday herald of the approaching Christmas season! There is light-brown ginger bread which is baked onto very thin wafers, Elisen with exotic oriental spices, dark honey ginger bread and dark-brown spice cookies with the flavor of cardamom. The visitor can admire, sniff at and taste all the ginger bread variations during the famous annual Christkindlesmarkt in the city of toys – Nuremberg. Who knows, Hänsel and Gretel may also be there.

2 eggs
1 cup sugar
1 cup flour
1/2 cup chopped almonds
3/4 cup grated almonds
2 tbsp. candied lemon peel, chopped
grated lemon peel (1 lemon)
2 pinches cinnamon
1 pinch ground cloves
1 pinch cardamom
16–20 thin wafers (Oblaten)
chocolate or sugar frosting

Beat eggs and sugar until foamy. Add flour, almonds, candied lemon peel, lemon peel and spices and mix thoroughly. Spread dough less than 1/4″ (1/2 cm) onto thin wafers. Bake in pre-heated 345°F (175°C) oven about 20 minutes. Cool and add either chocolate or sugar frosting. Note: ginger bread at first is rather hard. Put into tin can for a few weeks.

Odenwald Leg of Lamb

Hesse
(6 persons)

The Odenwald used to be a poor region and the food was quite simple. Whatever field and forest would provide was turned into a more or less appetizing meal. It was only during the last one hundred years that more refined foods have reached the remote valleys. Our lamb recipe, however, has enjoyed a long tradition.

3 1/2 lbs. leg of lamb
4 oz. bacon
For marinade:
1 1/4 cups vinegar
1 1/4 cups water
1 lemon, sliced
thyme, rosemary, 1 bunch greens, 1 onion
6 juniper berries, 1 clove garlic
2 1/2 cups red wine
For roasting:
salt
4 tbsp. butter
2 carrots
5 fl.oz. each of marinade, bouillon and sour cream
3 tbsp. flour

Bone meat, remove skin and fat. Lard (pierce) with bacon. Bring all ingredients of **marinade,** except wine, to boil and let steep 10 minutes. After cooling add wine. Put meat in appropriate bowl and pour marinade over it. Set aside 3 or 4 days, turn meat several times. Dry meat with paper towels and salt. In **roasting** pan melt butter, add carrots and sear meat on all sides. Add marinade and roast about two hours in oven at medium heat, occasionally add bouillon. 20 minutes before it is done brush meat with sour cream. At the end remove meat from pan, strain broth and bind with flour. Season gravy to taste and serve with potato croquettes and green butter beans.

Onion Pie

Swabia

The Chinese knew onions and many vegetables long before they reached the Occident. The onion first reached the Greeks and Romans by way of Babylon and the Romans brought it to Germania in the first century AD. It took until the late Middle Ages, however, to be accepted widely since its strong smell was too pungent for the times. And at court, eating onion was considered coarse and crude. How different today after the Swabians and their Alsatian neighbors invented a delectable recipe for onion pie, which is similar to a quiche.

For the yeast dough (pie crust):
4 cups flour
2 eggs
3 1/2 oz. (7 tbsp.) butter
1 pinch salt
5 fl.oz. milk
1 oz. compressed yeast or 2 tbsp. dry active yeast*
For onion filling:
2 1/2 lbs. onions, thinly sliced
2 oz. smoked bacon, diced
1 1/4 cups sour cream
4 eggs
5 tbsp. flour
1 pinch each of caraway seeds and salt

Combine ingredients for dough and allow to rise in warm place for 30 minutes. **For filling,** slice onion thinly, sauté without browning them. Fry bacon quickly and mix with sour cream, eggs, flour, caraway seeds, salt and combine with onions. Roll dough and place in large greased springform. Spread topping evenly on dough and bake in preheated 430°F (220°C) oven for approx. 1 hour till golden brown. Serve warm.

* Note: First mix yeast with 2 tbsp. milk and tsp. of sugar. Allow to rest 10 minutes before making dough.

Parfait of Broccoli

Lower Saxony

Broccoli is a close relative of cauliflower, but it is bushier and it is green. The umbels (that is the bushy part – in fact the flower) are light green to dark green. As soon as they start turning yellow Broccoli should not be consumed any more.

2 – 2 1/2 lbs. broccoli
1 small carrot
salt
5 eggs
1 cup cream
4 tbsp. grated Swiss cheese
1/4 tsp. nutmeg
white pepper
butter for greasing

Clean broccoli and carrot and boil slowly 15 minutes in salt water. Remove from liquid, set aside carrot. With exception of a few umbels purée broccoli in blender. Slowly add eggs, cream, cheese and spices to blender. Grease 6 custard cups 4″ dia. Fill with mixture. Put in oven into a shallow pan filled with water on low rack, bake at 285°F (140°C) for 70 minutes to solidify. Turn upside down on small plates. Garnish with carrot slices and broccoli. Serve hot immediately. Slices of smoked ham will not only please the eye but your palate, too.

Partridge "Wine Merchant"

Frankonia

It isn't surprising that an area as forested as Frankonia has to offer a cornucopia of excellent venison recipes. Be it in the Spessart Forest or in the Fichtel Mountains, the Frankonia Forest, the Rhön or Steiger Forest or the Frankonia Jura, one will encounter almost anything which will quicken the heart of the true venison gourmet – from the tangy Hasenpfeffer to the delicate partridge. And if you put the partridge in your pot, it won't be any longer in the tree!

4 young partridges
vine leaves
7 oz. smoked, sliced bacon
salt
clarified butter
small grapes
regular butter

Pluck partridges without injuring the skin. Do not wash inside. Cover partridges with vine leaves and wrap with bacon slices. Salt and bake about 20 minutes in 435°F (225°C) oven, using clarified butter. Glaze small grapes in hot butter. Serve with mashed potatoes. Arrange partridges on cabbage (see recipe page 176) but instead of 2 1/2 cups bouillon use 1 1/4 cup bouillon and white wine, each.

Paté du Chasseur

Westphalia

For paté lovers a recipe from a noble residence around the turn of the century.

For the dough:
1 2/3 cups flour
2 eggs, salt
4 oz. shortening
5 tbsp. water
For paté:
18 oz. venison (leg), cubed
10 oz. veal, cubed
7 oz. pork, cubed
8 oz. bacon slices
7 oz. chicken liver
2 1/2 tbsp. butter
salt, black pepper
1 tbsp. Madeira wine
2 tbsp. Provence or mixed spices
1/2 tsp. grated orange peel
1 tsp. sweet paprika
1 tsp. ground thyme
2 eggs
8 oz. bacon, cubed
1 egg yolk
butter for greasing pan

Mix ingredients for dough, knead thoroughly, form one lump and put in refrigerator 1 hour. **For paté:** Cool or freeze venison, veal, pork and bacon and purée in blender or food processor. Slice chicken livers, sauté in hot butter, season with salt and pepper, sprinkle Madeira on top. Allow to cool. Add salt, pepper, spices, orange peel, paprika, thyme, eggs and liver broth to paté meat and mix thoroughly. With rolling pin roll dough and line bottom and sides of greased paté form with 2/3 of dough. Line with bacon slices. Put 1/2 of paté mixture in paté pan, spread chicken liver on top and fill up with remaining half of paté mixture. Smooth top and place bacon slices on it. From remaining dough cut out shape for lid, seal seams with scrambled yolk. Cut 2 small holes in top for venting. Bake in 355–390°F (180–200°C) oven 90–120 minutes. Serve hot or cold.

Pike and Cheese Soufflé

Westphalia

At a time when creeks and streams were providing an ample supply of fish this recipe was born, using pike in sour cream, baked over with Parmesan cheese. The recipe is still in use although pike has become a rare and expensive delicacy. If you cannot locate pike, you can cook this soufflé with any other fish cutlet or fillet, such as cod or haddock etc. In those cases you don't have to allow as much for fish bone as with pike.

1 medium-size pike
salt, lemon juice
4 tbsp. butter
2–3 onions, chopped
1 tbsp. flour
2 1/2 cups sour cream
white pepper
4–5 tbsp. grated Parmesan

Prepare and gut fish, remove major (back-)bone, rinse thoroughly, dab dry and cut into 1 1/2" pieces. Salt and sprinkle with lemon juice. Heat butter in casserole, sauté onions till transparent, add fish pieces and cook until done. Remove fish and keep warm. Sauté flour in skillet until golden brown, add cream while stirring and pour sauce into heat-resistant casserole. Remove as many fish bones as possible, turn fish pieces in Parmesan and place into casserole. Sprinkle remaining cheese on top and bake in oven until golden brown. Serve with French bread (baguette) or boiled potatoes and salad.

Poached Egg
on
Leaf Spinach

Baden

We owe this Lenten fare to the Persians, for spinach came to our latitudes from their country around the year 1400. It is a wholesome winter vegetable whith which the recommended sauces should be used more sparingly. The Béchamel sauce was named after its creator, the Marquis Béchamel, who was a courtier at the court of Louis XIV. Therefore, we are in good company which is equal to the Imperial Persian spinach and the Royal Sauce Béchamel. (Recipe see Asparagus Casserole, page 34).

2 1/2 lbs. fresh leaf spinach
2 tbsp. onions, finely chopped
some butter, salt, garlic, nutmeg or pepper, vinegar
4 eggs
4 tbsp. Sauce Béchamel or Sauce hollandaise

Wash spinach leaves carefully and blanch for one minute in boiling water. Then chill quickly in very cold water and squeeze gently. Add onions to hot butter in frying pan, sauté till transparent, add and gently stir spinach in pan for very short time. Season with salt and, depending on taste, add garlic, pepper or nutmeg. Form four equal sized bases from spinach and place each on a seperate preheated platter. Slide into a boiling salt water/vinegar mixture four raw eggs, one after the other. Wait after each egg for water to boil again. Take pot from stove and allow the eggs four minutes before removing them. Place each egg on a separate spinach base, cover each with 1 tbsp. of sauce. Put into oven under broiler. A nice, light wine or rosé will heighten this palate's delight.

Pork Roulade
à la Baden

Baden

4 pork cutlets, approx. 5 oz. each
salt, pepper, mustard
1 clove of garlic
4 slices of smoked bacon
1 egg
7 oz. ground pork
3–4 carrots
some flour for dusting
some lard or shortening
2 onions
1 1/4 cups dry white wine
1/2 tbsp. whole black pepper
2 bay leaves
1 leek stalk
1/2 small celery root
3 tbsp. flour
5 fl.oz. sour cream
some butter

Pound the cutlets, season, spread mustard and 1/2 crushed clove of garlic on top and cover with bacon slices. Mix egg, salt and pepper with ground pork and spread on top of cutlets. Cut each carrot into four strips and press into ground meat. Roll up cutlets and secure with thread. Roll cutlets in flour and sear in hot lard or shortening for short time only. Remove from frying pan and put aside in saucepan. Fry the chopped onions golden brown, quickly stir in white wine and pour everything over roulades. Add the remaining garlic, the peppercorns, bay leaves and a touch of salt. Clean leek and celery root, cut into coarse strips and boil in lightly salted water till still crisp. Remove and strain. Add the salt water to roulades in saucepan and simmer for about one hour. Smoothly blend flour and sour cream, remove roulades from saucepan and bind sauce with the sour cream mixture. Stir while lightly boiling this gravy. Pass gravy through sieve onto roulades. Sauté vegetable strips and put them on top of roulades. Serve with Spätzle or noodles. Top with hot buttered bread crumbs.

Potato Pancakes and Apple Sauce

Hesse

Anyone being invited to potato pancakes better show some restraint or else he might be classified a "Nassauer". That is the German term for a sponger. It is no wonder that the good citizens of Nassau province suffer from this disgraceful name, for it is they who were sponged on. As it happened, in the good old days of the Student Prince, the Duke of Nassau supported twelve "free tables" in the Göttingen University cafeteria for less privileged students of his Duchy. But soon other students helped themselves at the Hesse-Nassau tables to a free meal, enjoying the sport of "nassauering".

2 1/4 lbs. potatoes
2 eggs
salt
1 onion, grated
lard or shortening
1 lb. apple sauce
crème fraîche or sour cream

Pare raw potatoes, grate and squeeze out liquid through cheese-cloth. Add eggs, salt and grated onion, mix thoroughly. Melt fat in skillet and fry small, thin pancakes crisply from both sides. Use plenty of apple sauce at the table. A delicacy for which "nassauering" will be forgiven! Serve with crème fraîche (or sour cream) and water cress.

Potato Salad

Swabia

The Swabians have a reputation as inventors and philosophers. They are said to possess copyright protection on liberalism, mineral water, Spätzle, the automobile, the Zeppelin, Mr. Einstein and potato salad. Every Swabian housewife probably prefers her own brand of potato. Whatever it is, it never is a soft, mushy potato but a type that stays firm even after boiling and slicing. Since the great majority of German immigrants to America are native Swabians, they brought back the potato to its native land in the form of potato salad. You can best enjoy it with one of its preferred complementary dishes, Leberkäs (recipe see page 16) and a cool glass of beer.

8 medium size, firm potatoes
1 onion, finely chopped
vinegar of wine
salt
sunflower or safflower oil
white, ground pepper
some warm bouillon

Boil potatoes in their skin, peel and allow to cool a little. Slice and add onion. Add vinegar, salt, oil, pepper and hot bouillon. Mix well – the salad ought to be quite moist.

Potato Soup and Bacon

Westphalia

One cannot find more potato recipes than in West-phalia. This lively soup is one of them – even potato haters will like it. Potatoes only became a popular food in the second half of the 18th century. Housewives first had to learn how to prepare these new tubers. Cookbooks gave the necessary suggestions – such as a 1797 book with the title: "Economical-practical lessons on the advantageous cultivation and best use of potatoes". Our potato soup is one of the recipes listed except that it was later refined through the addition of bacon instead of browned butter.

1 1/4 lbs. potatoes
1 tsp. salt
1/2 tsp. caraway seeds
1 onion, diced
1 1/2 tbsp. lard or butter
2 tbsp. flour
white pepper, 1 pinch marjoram
3/4 cup smoked bacon, diced
5 fl.oz. sour cream
1/2 bunch parsley, finely chopped

Pare potatoes and cube, boil in 2 1/2 cups salt water and caraway seeds until almost done. Meanwhile, sauté onion in lard or butter until golden yellow, add flour, slightly brown it and add water from boiling potatoes. Season with pepper and marjoram, boil quickly and add potatoes. Mix well and simmer until potatoes are soft. Dice bacon, sauté well and add to soup including liquid fat. Refine with sour cream, season to taste and add parsley.

Prune Pie

Palatinate

There are probably as many recipe variations on prune pie as there are German provinces. We have chosen the one from the Palatinate for its relative simplicity and tastiness. The Palatinate and Baden are the provinces with the most bountiful prune orchards and it is no wonder that theirs appear to be the juiciest pies. A prudent housewife always preserves plenty of prunes in fall to have a year-around supply for making this delicious pie.

3 1/2 cups flour
3/4 cups lukewarm milk
1 1/2 oz. compressed yeast or 3 tbsp. active dry yeast
7 oz. butter, soft
2 eggs
1/2 cup sugar
1 tsp. salt
grease for baking sheet
4 1/2 lbs. prunes, quite ripe
sugar and cinnamon mixture for spreading on pie

Mix half the flour with the milk and yeast. Allow to rise, then add remaining flour and soft butter, eggs, sugar and salt. Allow to rise again and roll out on floured bread board rather thinly. Place on greased cooky sheet. Pit the prunes by cutting lenghtwise so as to obtain a one-piece open prune. (Prune pitters are available in German stores that make pitting a nifty operation). Place prunes face up on dough, overlapping them like roof shingles. Allow to rest a short time and put in oven at medium heat until dough is nice and crisp. Sprinkle sugar and cinnamon over pie.
Note: this yeast dough is universally used for many German fruit pie crusts.

Purée of Peas

Frankonia

Peas are the most widely consumed leguminous vegetable in Europe. They are rich in vitamins and proteins but also in carbohydrates and that also makes them rich in calories. They came to Europe 4000 years BC via the Balkan peninsula together with other cultivated plants. The rule of Charlemagne also marks the period during which peas made their way and acceptance into German kitchens. Before that time they were an exotic rarity, and it took until the 19th century before peas became a popular staple.

2 cups dried green or yellow peas
4–6 cups water
1 bunch greens (parsley, celery, carrots, leek)
For gravy:
1 onion, sliced in rings
2–3 tbsp. butter or shortening
2–3 tbsp. flour
1 pinch salt, 1 pinch pepper
1/2 cup bacon, diced

Day before: wash peas and soak overnight. Clean greens, chop and add to peas.
About 2 hours before serving: Boil peas and vegetables slowly for 1 to 1 1/2 hours (depending on softness of peas). Press soft peas and vegetables through sieve or purée in blender. For **gravy,** heat onion rings in saucepan in fat, add flour and sauté until light brown. Add mashed peas, bring to slow boil while stirring constantly. Season to taste with salt and pepper. To serve, sauté diced bacon and sprinkle over top. This is an ideal side dish to many of the meat dishes in this book.

Ragout of Hare

Baden

This recipe should actually be called "Ragout of hare seasoned with (or in) pepper". By the way, peppery ragout containing breast, head, neck, liver, heart and lung of hare was one of Casanova's favorite dishes. Anyone familiar with Casanova's amorous adventures will suspect why he consumed this "aphrodisian Hasenpfeffer" so frequently.

1 whole, freshly hunted hare
Marinade:
2 cups red wine
2 whole cloves
1 bay leaf
1 onion
1 carrot
1 leek stalk
1/2 small celery root
1 garlic clove
some parsley

shortening
1 tbsp. tomato paste
flour for dusting
1 cup bouillon or consommée of beef
pepper

Cut up the hare into pieces, including bones, liver, heart and lung. Prepare **marinade** from red wine, spices and vegetables and allow hare to soak in it for two days in refrigerator in covered pan. Afterwards put meat on a strainer and keep marinade. Braise meat in frying pan from all sides in heated fat. Add vegetables from marinade and tomato paste and sauté alongside meat. Dust meat with flour and add bouillon. Allow to simmer for 1–1 1/2 hours until meat is done. Remove bones and keep meat in covered dish. Season the gravy with ground pepper, slowly add the marinade but do not allow to boil. Pour this gravy over meat through fine-meshed sieve. Ideal side dishes are mushrooms, glazed chestnuts, cranberries, noodles. A dry, heavy Pinot Noir wine will add the finishing touch to this country squire's meal.

Ragout of Lamb Rhenania

Rhineland

An old cookbook says: "lamb is the strongest and most nourishing meat after beef. It can be highly recommended to the weak and to convalescents provided the fat is cut away to keep it from weighing heavily in the stomach with its unpleasant taste". It wasn't until too long ago that sheep herders were grazing their itinerant herds on the Rhine meadows near the centers of big cities. People in the Rhine area like their lamb well seasoned.

2 1/2 lbs. shoulder of lamb
2 oz. bacon, diced
2 oz. smoked, lean bacon, diced
2 onions, cubed
1 clove of garlic
5 tomatoes
1/2 tsp. confectioner's sugar
1 1/2 tsp. salt
1 tsp. pepper
1 1/2 tbsp. flour
2 1/2 cups bouillon
1 tbsp. Madeira wine

Cut meat in 1″–1 1/2″ cubes. Dice bacon and melt in skillet. Add meat and sear. Cube onions, crush garlic and add to meat for last ten minutes. Reduce heat. Scald tomatoes quickly with hot water, peel and quarter, add to meat. Sprinkle sugar, pepper and flour on meat and stir. Add bouillon and allow to simmer, covered, approx. 1 1/2 hours. Add Madeira and serve with green beans and boiled potatoes. If you prefer, garnish with hard boiled egg halves.

Ragout of Veal

Westphalia

This ragout, like Ragoût Fin, is usually served as an hors d'œuvre but you can make a regular meal of it, if you serve the ragout (without the paté shell) with boiled potatoes and fresh salad. You can also use venison with this recipe.

1 3/4 lbs. veal, diced
1 1/4 cups white wine
2 tbsp. vinegar
5 juniper berries
2 oz. bacon, diced
1 tbsp. butter
5 tbsp. flour
1 tbsp. tomato paste
1 1/4 cups bouillon
4 tbsp. cream
salt, black pepper
12 oz. mushrooms, sliced
1 scallion, finely chopped
2 tbsp. butter
4 paté shells (from store)
lemon, sliced in 1/8 slices
1 bunch parsley, chopped
Worcestershire Sauce

Night before: Dice veal and marinate overnight in mixture of wine, vinegar and crushed juniper berries.
Strain meat and dab dry. Save marinade. Sear meat and bacon in hot butter. Dust with flour and brown. Mix tomato paste, bouillon and cream and add to meat. Stir and bring to quick boil, simmer for 45 minutes at medium to low heat. Add 5 fl.oz. from strained marinade, heat quickly but do not boil. Season with salt and pepper. Strain mushrooms. Sauté scallion in butter until transparent, add mushrooms and sauté for 20 minutes. Fold mixture into meat. Heat paté shells in oven and fill with ragout. Garnish with lemon slices and parsley. Season with Worcestershire Sauce.

Red Currant Pie

Swabia

The Swabian housewife as a confectioner or a producer of cookies is a story all by itself, because it takes a great deal of experience, calls for a lot of labor and is, in the end, a very unthankful enterprise – whatever is delectable will disappear quickly. Try this recipe and you will make the same experience. Red currant in German is Johannisbeeren, "St. John's berries", because they usually mature around St. John's Day.

For dough: (pie crust)
1 1/2 cups flour
1 tsp. baking powder
4 oz. butter or margarine
1/2 cup sugar
2 egg yolks
grated peel of 1/2 lemon
For topping:
2 egg whites
1/2 cup sugar
2 tsp. cornstarch
1 1/8 lbs. red currants (wash and remove little stems)

Sift flour and baking powder together and mix with butter, sugar, egg yolks and lemon peel. Rest dough in cool place for 30 minutes. Roll and put into spring form. Bake at medium heat till golden yellow for approx. 25 minutes. **For topping:** Meanwhile, beat egg whites stiff, add sugar and cornstarch and beat another 5 minutes. Now fold in red currants. Spread everything evenly on top of pie crust and bake in medium oven until light yellow. It will be delicious!

Red Grits Pudding

Frisia

Rote Grütze is also a favorite dessert in Southern Germany. But its origin lies buried in the High North, Schleswig-Holstein and Denmark. Up North they used to call almost every type of grits or porridge "red grits" if it was boiled with fruit juices instead of water. There are many widely differing recipes. Some housewives swear that they taste best with fresh fruit, others think they should be made from fruit juices even during harvest time.

1 quart fruit juice (diluted) of red currant, raspberry or rhubarb
sugar to taste
6 tbsp. cornstarch
milk

Bring fruit juice to slow boil. Add sugar to taste. Make thin paste from starch and add to slowly boiling fruit juice. Keep stirring and boil slowly for 5 minutes. Pour into glass bowl. Serve with cold milk or light cream after it has solidified or cooled.

Rhine Pike à la Baden

Baden

This voracious fresh water fish, weighing up to seven pounds, can be turned into one of the finest dishes from among the denizens of the river realm. Since its meat tends to be dry, it is best to steam or stew the whole fish. Connoisseurs savor its liver as a delicacy.

Approx. 2 1/2 lbs. of pike
pepper, salt, some flour
2 tbsp. butter
2 tbsp. diced onion
1 bunch of parsley
lemon juice
1 1/4 cups of fresh cream
1 tbsp. (veal) bottled sauce for gravy

Scale, gut and wash the fish. Carefully rub with salt and pepper. Dust lightly with flour and sauté until golden yellow. Arrange fish in such a manner that it will lie naturally on its belly in an open casserole and allow to cook in pre-heated 390°F–430°F (200°–220°C) oven. When almost done add a little butter to pan and sauté onions until glossy. Take pike from oven in pan and sprinkle profusely with finely chopped parsley and lemon juice. Add cream to base in casserole and mix thoroughly. Pour this liquid repeatedly over fish on top of stove to obtain a regular gravy. To get an appetizingly brown color, add 1 tbsp. of veal gravy to it. Homemade noodles and a light, dry Riesling or rosé wine will go well with this meal.

River Main Pike
in Sour Cream

Frankonia

Even Imperial Rome knew environmental and ecological problems. A pike, for instance, in order to be considered edible, had to be caught "between the two bridges", i.e. inside the section delineated between the Tiber Isle and the confluence with the main sewage canal. One not only had to know how to bait this exclusive predatory fish but also where to catch it. Unfortunately, the problems existing in the Tiber River more than 2000 years ago still exist today in many other rivers of the world.

1 pike 3–3 1/2 lbs.
4 oz. smoked bacon
salt, lemon, some flour
clarified butter
2 1/2 cups dry white wine (Frankonia)
bottled or canned beef gravy
1 cup sour cream

Wash cleaned pike, fillet, skin and remove all bones. Lard fillets with slivers of smoked bacon (as shown in photograph), season with salt and lemon, dust with flour. Braise fillets quickly in butter and add white wine. Allow fish to stew for 20 minutes in this broth. Remove fillets and arrange on preheated platter. Add bottled gravy and sour cream to broth. Bring to short boil, season to taste and pour over fillets. Serve with boiled potatoes and cucumber salad with dill.

Roast,
Hunter's Delight

Hesse

The most important part of this recipe is the
marinade in which the meat is steeped for at least
two days. Do not be parsimonious in the wrong
place. The red wine should not be of the ordinary
table wine classification. A fine Pinot Noir would
be quite fitting. And wine vinegar is "de rigueur"
because its acid is derived exclusively from wine
spirits and small additions of tartaric acid. Boneless Boston butt pork shoulder roast is the meat of
your choice.

For marinade:
3 3/4 cups water
1 1/2 cups red wine
1 1/2 cups wine vinegar
4 oz. celery stalk, cubed
4 oz. carrots, sliced
1 stalk leek, sliced
6 juniper berries
2 cloves, crushed
1 tsp. basil
1 heaping tsp. salt
lemon peel from 1 lemon
2 small twigs of fir

3 1/2 lbs. pork (Boston butt shoulder, boneless)
4 tbsp. shortening
5 fl.oz. cream
2 tbsp. cranberries or cranberry sauce

Put all **marinade** ingredients and meat in crock or
bowl for 2–3 days, cover meat with fir twigs. After
marinating remove meat and dry well.
Heat shortening in roasting pan and sear on all
sides. Add marinade and roast for abt. 90 minutes
at medium heat. Baste frequently. Remove meat,
keep warm while passing broth through sieve and
adding cream. Bring gravy to quick boil. Serve
with cranberries. Boiled or mashed potatoes and
red cabbage will add the finishing touch.

Rolled Kidney of Veal Roast

Bavaria
(for 8 persons)

Gourmets have always savored kidneys because of their tenderness and delicate taste. The kidneys should be from very young animals, preferably sold on the day of butchering for maximum taste.

3 1/2 lbs. boned veal kidney roast, including kidneys
(or 3 lbs. veal rib or loin roast + 3/4 lb. veal kidneys)
lemon juice, salt, pepper
4 tbsp. shortening
2 onions
1 bunch soup greens (parsley, celery, chives etc.)
1 piece of bread rind
2 1/2 cups hot water
1 tbsp. flour
5 tbsp. sour cream

Wash meat, remove all skin and rub cutting edges with lemon juice. Halve kidneys, rub meat with salt and pepper and place kidney halves on top of meat, roll up tightly and tie with twine. Melt fat in roasting pan and sear meat on all sides. Quarter onions, chop greens, split bone in two and put everything including bread rind into pan and fry quickly, add the hot water. Put in 390°F (200°C) pre-heated oven for approx. 2 hours, basting often with its broth. Turn meat frequently to obtain browning on all sides. Strain broth, bind with flour, add sour cream, season to taste. Serve with mashed potatoes and fresh vegetables.

Roulade of Cabbage

Frankonia

Cabbage is said to have been a popular staple among the Anglo-Saxons in the 5th century. But the Romans must have known it, too, because they named it "caput" from which the words Kappus or Kappes were formed. They are still in use in a number of German provinces.

1 head of cabbage
1 lb. ground pork (or pork + beef)
1 onion, minced
salt, pepper, nutmeg
4 slices bacon
4 eggs

Boil cabbage for five minutes. Remove from water and separate leaves. Combine ground meat, onion, eggs and some water and season with salt, pepper and nutmeg. Roll abt. 4 oz. of ground meat into 3 to 4 cabbage leaves, put one slice of bacon on top of each roulade and stew in covered saucepan about one hour. Serve with mashed potatoes.

Rüdesheim Apple Casserole

Hesse

Rüdesheim, the famous wine village along the Rhine River, surely has not made history because of its apple casserole but because it is picturesquely situated on the right river bank with charming little streets and alleys and where a great deal of the fermented grape juice is consumed – sometimes in excess – especially in the well-known Drosselgasse. And "if you don't like wine, women and song – you stay a fool your whole life long". We have taken a glass full of the former and put it in this recipe.

1 quart milk
pinch of salt
3–4 tbsp. butter
4–5 tbsp. sugar
1 envelope vanilla-flavored sugar or 1 tsp. vanilla extract
2/3 cup semolina (cream of wheat)
2 1/4 lbs. apples
1 cup white wine
juice of one lemon
4 tbsp. sugar
3–4 tbsp. raisins, soaked in water
4 egg whites
4 tbsp. cream
4 egg yolks
granulated sugar, cinnamon

Bring milk to boil. Add salt, butter, sugar, vanilla and semolina while stirring constantly. Allow to sit on burner 10 minutes at very low heat. Meanwhile, pare and core apples, cut in thin slices and place in bowl. Pour white wine, lemon juice and sugar over them. Finely chop soaked raisins and add to apples. Beat egg whites stiff. Fold into semolina mixture, combine with cream, egg yolks and prepared apples carefully and put into casserole. Bake in 355°F (180°C) oven about 40 minutes. Before serving sprinkle with a mixture of granulated sugar and cinnamon. Serve with a vanilla sauce.

Rum Custard

Frisia

Most people believe rum is for drinking only. But this dessert recipe proves that rum is not only fortifying in the liquid state. True, the dessert is on the heavy side but if you can't even think of food after a wholesome meal you may want to leave out the whipped cream. It still tastes delectably without it.

2 1/2 cups milk
1/4 length of whole vanilla or 1/2 tsp. vanilla extract
4 egg yolks
3/4 cup sugar
2 tbsp. Knox unflavored gelatin (see instructions below)
rum to taste (minimum a small wine glass)
1 1/4 cups whipping cream
4 egg whites, beaten stiff

Combine cold milk and vanilla in one pan on stove. In double-boiler pan without heat, stir egg yolk and sugar until foamy and slowly add to milk after milk starts boiling. Return this mixture to double-boiler pan, heat and beat until it has consistency of pudding. Turn off heat, stir until it has cooled and add the dissolved gelatin and the rum. Fold in stiff egg whites and whipped cream carefully and, as soon as mixture begins to stiffen, pour into glass bowl. After it has cooled completely you may top it with whipped cream.

Gelatin instructions: In small saucepan dissolve gelatin in 4 tbsp. cold water, let stand 10 minutes then heat while stirring (do not boil) until fluid is clear. Allow to cool to room temperature and add to pudding while stirring.

Sauerbraten

Rhineland

This recipe needs no translation. When Americans think of German food they most likely think of Sauerkraut, Sauerbraten and Bratwurst, in that order. The truth is that neither of them is consumed in excess in Germany. They are simply one of many German meals. It is true, however, that Sauerkraut was consumed in great quantities among the general – and poor – population in the last few centuries.

2 1/2 cups water
1 1/4 cups wine vinegar
2 onions, finely chopped
1/2 celery root, chopped
1 carrot, sliced
10 peppercorns
2 juniper berries
2 whole cloves
1 bay leaf
2 1/4 lbs. beef
1 tsp. salt
1/2 tsp. pepper
5 tbsp. raisins
3 1/2 oz. butter
1 tbsp. tomato paste
1 tbsp. almonds, chopped
1 tsp. cornstarch

Boil water and vinegar with onions, celery, carrot and spices. Allow to cool and pour over meat in pan. Cover and set aside in cool place for 2–3 days. Turn meat occasionally. Remove from marinade, dry and rub with salt and pepper. Soak raisins in cold water. Heat fat in pan and sear meat on all sides. Strain marinade and sauté vegetables in same pan with meat. Stir in tomato paste and add half of heated marinade. Allow to simmer, covered, for abt. 2 hours at medium heat. Remove meat and keep warm. Add remaining marinade to broth and stir. Strain and quickly boil again with raisins and almonds, thicken with cornstarch. Slice meat, serve with gravy and potato dumplings (recipe see page 42).

Sauerkraut

Swabia

It is taken for granted that almost any German housewife knows how to prepare a hearty sauerkraut. It's probably for that reason that Anglo-Saxons call us "Krauts". Or is it because of envy?

1 onion, minced
3 tbsp. of lard or goose-fat or regular shortening
one shot each of bouillon and white wine
1 3/4 lbs. of sauerkraut*
1 tbsp. juniper berries
1 goodly pinch each of caraway seed, thyme and marjoram
1/2 bay leaf
1 tbsp. flour

Sauté onion in fat, light brown, add bouillon and wine. Add sauerkraut and simmer 30–40 minutes, covered. About halfway add juniper berries and bay leaf. Toward end shake flour and a little cold water in shaker and add.

You can definitely improve taste if you add a few sides of bacon to simmering phase, and, if available, home-made liverwurst. Serve with the inevitable Spätzle or boiled potatoes. (Recipe see page 184).

* Note: American sauerkraut is often very salty. We recommend rinsing it in cold water several times before cooking it.

Sauerkraut Casserole

Palatinate

This is a typical Monday dish because you can use leftovers and the poor housewife can take a breather after a family-intensive weekend. It will sizzle all by its little self once put in the oven. The simplicity of preparing this meal bears no relation to its savory taste.

1 onion, diced
2 tbsp. butter
3/4 lb. ground beef or beef/pork mixture
salt, pepper
grease for pan
mashed potatoes from 2 1/4 lbs. potatoes
1 lb. sauerkraut, raw or cooked
1 tbsp. butter

Dice onion and in skillet sauté in butter. Add ground meat and fry at high heat while stirring to make meat crumbly, add salt and pepper. Remove from heat. Grease baking pan. Spread one layer of mashed potatoes, add a layer of sauerkraut. Add a good layer of ground beef. Repeat in that order until pan is full. The top layer must be mashed potatoes. Place a few flakes of butter on top and put in pre-heated oven at medium heat for 45 minutes.

Note: American canned sauerkraut is rather strongly salted. You may want to soak it for 1/2 hour before using it.

Sausages on Cabbage Bavarian Style

Bavaria

It is said that Bratwurst was already available around 1530 in the town of Coburg. One hundred years later Duke Casimir passed a tax ordinance decreeing that Bratwurst must not cost more than 4 1/2 Pfennige and four of them must weigh one pound. Today the heavy smell of Bratwurst still wafts around the Coburg market square. The secret of this Coburg specialty rests in the composition of the ground meat filling and the particular seasoning of it, and, of course, the way they are barbecued over a fire fueled by pine cones.

1 head of cabbage
3 tbsp. lard or shortening
1 tbsp. sugar
1 onion, diced
1 apple (unpared) sliced
1 pinch salt and pepper, each
2 1/2 cups bouillon or beef consommée
2 tbsp. vinegar
8 link sausages
shortening for frying

Wash cabbage and cut out stem. Cut cabbage in slivers. Melt lard in pot and brown sugar in it lightly. Add onion and apple slices and sauté quickly. Add cabbage, season with salt and pepper and pour bouillon over it. Allow to cook on low heat for approx. one hour, stirring occasionally. Toward end add vinegar. Fry sausages either in frying pan or barbecue after brushing with oil. A hearty brick oven bread and a glass of beer will bring Bavaria right in your living room.

Schales

Palatinate

This was originally a Jewish dish which the Palatinates gleaned from their Jewish neighbours. It is the Palatinate version of Schalet or Scholet, a stew which was prepared on Fridays and served on Sabbath on which no Jew is supposed to work. The Palatinate citizens replaced Jewish kosher meat with smoked bacon. Even Heinrich Heine, the Jewish-German poet liked to mention his taste for Schales.

2 lbs. potatoes, grated
3–4 stalks leek, sliced
2 eggs
salt and pepper
grease for stew pan
1/2 lb. smoked bacon, diced

Grate raw potatoes on coarse potato grater. Slice leek in thin slices. Mix with potatoes, add eggs, seasoning and smoked bacon. Put mixture into greased pan and bake in pre-heated oven for 1 1/2 hours at medium heat. Lamb's lettuce with vinegar-oil dressing is the recommended salad.

Schneckennudeln

Palatinate

Here is another culinary nomenclature that defies translation. Literally it means "snails' noodles" but it contains neither. The term snail refers to the "snailed-up" shape like a snail in its little portable house. Noodle is just a generalized term that should not be taken too narrowly. It is really a pastry specialty based on yeast dough.

1 2/3 cups flour
1/2 tsp. salt
1 egg
1 1/2 oz. compressed yeast or 3 tbsp. active dry yeast
1/4 lb. butter
1 1/2 tbsp. oil
2–3 tbsp. sugar
1 package vanilla flavored sugar or 1 tsp. vanilla extract
grated peel of 1 lemon
For filling:
2 cups ground hazelnuts
3 1/2 tbsp. butter
3 tbsp. sugar
1 shot of milk
2/3 cup raisins
5 tbsp. clear brandy (from apple, pear, prune etc.)
1 1/2 cups confectioner's sugar

Mix and beat flour, salt, egg, yeast*, butter and oil. Put this lump of dough into bowl of cold water. When the lump floats, allow to float 5 minutes and remove from water. Now add sugar, vanilla and lemon peel. Beat again thoroughly. Roll dough on floured bread board with rolling pin. **For filling,** spread mix from hazelnuts, butter, sugar, milk and raisins on top of dough. Roll up dough and cut slices abt. 1 1/4″ and place them into 8″ or 9″ buttered springform. Allow to rest 1/2 hour at room temperature. Bake in pre-heated, medium heat oven 1/2 hour. Mix brandy and confectioner's sugar and brush on baked cake while hot.

* Note: It is recommended that yeast be dissolved in 2 tbsp. lukewarm milk and 1/2 tbsp. sugar 5–10 minutes before adding to dough.

Shrimp Cocktail Husum

Frisia

The greatest among the small delicacies along the West Coast of Jutland to this day are its shrimps. North Sea shrimp, of course, are much smaller than the American variety, the shrimp or prawn from the Gulf of Mexico but their delicate meat is equal to any. In the old days the reddish-brown delectables had to be brought to market rather quickly, but ever since the turn of century it has been possible to conserve them safely. They taste best when fresh, however, especially if you can buy them portside directly from the small fishing boats right out of their steaming kettles.

8 tbsp. mayonnaise
1 tbsp. tomato ketchup
1 dash Worcestershire Sauce
some lemon juice, salt, pepper
1/2 lb. shrimps
12 olive halves, filled
1 banana, cubed
parsley, minced

Mix mayonnaise, ketchup and Worcestershire sauce and season to taste. Carefully fold in shrimps and banana cubes. Fill into proper glasses, garnish with parsley and lemon slices.

Spätzle

Swabia

Swabians and Spätzle are as inseparable as Bavarians and dumplings or French and French bread or Swedes and smörgåsbord. They are praised in song and poem and we offer the Anglicized version of such an 1838 masterpiece by an unknown author. Perhaps he should remain unknown:

Oh, come and watch our kitchen maid
How she prepares the dough without much aid
She spreads it on a little wooden board
And scrapes them, not too long and not too short
The input is, I say, just eggs and flour
A little lukewarm water, nothing sour
The Swabian Spätzle are quite inexpensive
Which makes their value even more extensive.

1 2/3 cups flour
3 eggs
1 tsp. salt
5 fl.oz. water (added till right consistency)
For topping:
1 tbsp. butter
1 tbsp. dried bread crumbs

Make a smooth, tough dough, using wooden spoon or hand-held mixer by adding to flour eggs, salt and lukewarm water in increments till right consistency is reached. Spread portions of dough on wooden (Spätzle-)board and scrape with special scraper (shown) or wide knife, slivers of dough into rapidly boiling salt water. As soon as Spätzle rise to surface remove with skimmer (shown), drop them in hot water and immediately place them in colander to drain. Arrange on heated platter.

For **topping** on Spätzle, heat butter in skillet and add dry bread crumbs, stir till fried golden brown. Spread on top of Spätzle platter.

Note: Instead of "scraping" Spätzle, the easier and just as effective way is to press dough through a special Spätzle maker.

Note: Water should be boiling rapidly at all times. Remove Spätzle when they rise to top *and* when water looks frothy on top.

Spicy Beef Pot-au-Feu

Westphalia

Pfefferpotthast is the favourite Dortmund dish. It is even served at official municipal receptions and could be bought on market days as early as the 14th century. During that time, the Free Imperial City of Dortmund was besieged by Count von der Mark. A Dortmund lady, Agnetta von Vierbecke tried to smuggle enemy soldiers into town hidden under hay and logs of wood. She tried to persuade the guards at the city gate to allow the "Trojan wagons" free passage and to buy her a meal of Potthast. The ruse failed, however, and Agnetta was burned at the stake.

2 1/2 lbs. beef (rib or chuck) cubed
1 3/4 lbs. onions, sliced
5 tbsp. lard or clarified butter
1 quart bouillon
1 tsp. whole peppercorns, salt
2 bay leaves
4 whole cloves
2 tbsp. dried bread crumbs
lemon juice
1 tbsp. capers

Cube meat in bite-size pieces. Sauté onions in large skillet in hot fat. Add meat and sear quickly, add salt, bouillon, peppercorns, bay leaves and cloves. Cover and allow to simmer 1 1/2 hours at low heat. Add bread crumbs, stir and cook another 5 minutes. Add lemon juice and capers, season with salt and pepper. Serve with potatoes and gherkins.

Stream Trout and Crayfish

Lower Saxony

Even though the times have long gone by when children were able to catch trout and crayfish with their bare hands out of streams, it is still possible to afford these culinary pleasures, today. Your guests are unlikely to forget this light exquisite dish.

4 trouts, 1/2 lb. each, gutted
1 quart water
1 bunch fresh dill
1 shot white wine
12 live fresh water crayfish
3 quarts water, salt
1 bunch fresh dill and dill seed
For the sauce:
2 tbsp. butter
4 tbsp. flour
2 1/2 cups water from boiling crayfish
1 tbsp. meat extract or butter gravy
lemon juice from 1/2 lemon
4 tbsp. cream
salt, white pepper
1 pinch granulated sugar
dill for garnish

Tie each trout, head to tail. Simmer in salt water-dill-wine mixture. Remove from water and keep warm. Drop crayfish into rapidly boiling salt water and boil slowly for 15 minutes together with the dill. Allow to cool. Remove meat from claws and tails and cube meat from tails. Pulverize shells in mortar. **For the sauce:** In skillet heat butter and sauté pulverized shells until butter turns reddish. Stir and add flour. Add water from boiling crayfish. Boil and strain. Add meat extract, lemon juice and cream, season to taste. Arrange trout on pre-heated plates. Pour sauce over them. Garnish with dill. Serve with boiled potatoes and melted butter.

Stuffed Wild Duck with Blueberry Patties

Baden

In the duck family the wild duck is the real delicacy.

4 breasts of wild duck
7 oz. goose liver paste
grapes as desired
4 slices of bacon
Patties:
5 medium-sized potatoes
5 fl.oz. cream
2–3 egg yolks
salt, pepper
1 tsp. chopped ginger root
1 cup (4 oz.) blueberries
1 tbsp. butter
3 tbsp. olive oil
1 1/4 cups bottled or canned beef gravy
Purée:
1 lb. parsley root
salt, nutmeg
1 1/4 cups cream
2 tbsp. butter

Cut small pockets into breasts of duck from top to bottom. Cut goose liver paste into wide strips and stuff into pockets together with grapes. Wrap each breast with a slice of bacon and secure with thread. Boil pared potato strips in salt water, strain and allow to cool somewhat. Press through potato masher or sieve. Add cream, egg yolk and season. Allow to cool. Sauté the prepared duck breasts in a little butter and one tbsp. olive oil at low heat. Season with salt and pepper when turning them. Heat remaining olive oil in another pan and put small heaps of the mashed potato mix in it with a tablespoon. Flatten a little and place a teaspoon full of blueberries on top. Bake in pre-heated oven at 390°F (200°C) as desired. Remove duck breasts from pan, prepare gravy by adding bottled gravy to fluid in pan. Pare parsley root, boil in salt water and purée in mixer together with cream. Season, heat with a little butter.

Swabian
Filled Noodles

Swabia

Although the Swabians are stout believers, some-times called "Pietists", they did not wish to give up meat during Lenten season. So they had to invent a ruse to hide the meat from the Good Lord. The result is Maultaschen and whether these giant ravioli are supposed to be made with or without spinach is an argument that will probably never be settled.

For dough: (in Germany you can buy rolled dough from your bakery)
1 lb. flour
4 eggs, pinch of salt
For filling:
12 oz. mixture of veal, beef and smoked bacon in equal parts, blended (you can buy this mixture as "Brät" in German butcher shops)
1 onion, 1/2 stalk leek, parsley – all finely chopped
4 stale rolls
1/2 lb. frozen spinach, creamed
3 eggs
salt, nutmeg, pepper

Heap flour on bread board, add eggs and salt into a dip in flour. Knead well to obtain smooth, tough dough and separate into 6 equal round lumps. With rolling pin roll each paper-thin to form approx. 7" rectangles. **For filling:** Cool or freeze meat before puréeing in blender or food processor. Sauté onions, leek and parsley. Soak rolls and squeeze out by hand. Combine everything with defrosted spinach, eggs and season with spices. Mix well. Now spread filling down the middle of each strip of dough, leave end free for sealing. Brush one edge with water or egg white, fold over and seal. Cut this "tube" into equal pieces abt. 2 1/2 – 3" wide and boil in bouillon 10 to 15 minutes. Serve as shown. Or, next day, cut in slices and fry with eggs, then serve with potato salad (recipe see page 138).

Swabian Ragout of Veal

Swabia

Theodor Heuss, the first President of the Federal Republic, never could nor wanted to disclaim his Swabian heritage. The charming old gentleman was also very open-minded and enlightened toward physical pleasures. "It is not very likely to find another mild dish outside of Swabia like the one we call 'pickled veal' – boiled veal with a sautéed white sauce". And, indeed, it is a recipe which is hardly known outside of Swabia but which is well worth to be introduced to a broader and appreciative public.

1 3/4 lbs. veal, shoulder or blade
1 bunch soup greens
1 pinch salt
1 onion
1 lemon slice
6 cups water
For the sauce:
2 tbsp. butter
1/2 cup flour
2 1/2 cups (veal) broth
juice from 1/4 lemon
1 1/4 cups white wine
5–10 fl.oz. of cream
1 egg yolk

Cut meat to bite-size cubes and add to boiling water together with soup greens, salt, onion and lemon slice. Simmer till tender. **For the sauce:** Now heat butter in skillet, add flour until light brown, then add veal broth. Boil slowly for short time while stirring. Add remaining ingredients – except the egg yolk – and meat. Allow to boil for short time. Remove from heat and slowly add yolk. Serve immediately with Spätzle (recipe see page 184) and a nice salad.

Swabian Roastbeef

Swabia

The so-called Fildern is a relatively small, fertile area to the South of Stuttgart. It is here, right in the heart of Swabia that one of the best varieties of cabbage in Germany is grown. It is known as Filderkraut and many dyed-in-the-wool Swabians prefer it, together with a real roast beef, to all the culinary specialties of the world.

1 onion, sliced
3 oz. smoked bacon, diced
3 oz. lard or shortening
2 1/2 lbs. sauerkraut
salt, pepper, oil
juniper berries
caraway seeds, white pepper
some bouillon
sugar
some white wine
4 tbsp. butter
4 onions, sliced
4 slices of beef, abt. 7 oz. each and abt. 3/4" thick

Fry one onion and bacon in large skillet or pan till golden brown. Spread sauerkraut on top, season. Add berries and seeds and stir. Add some bouillon, water and allow to simmer 1 to 1 1/2 hours until soft. During last 15 minutes add a little sugar and some white wine. Meanwhile, in skillet sauté four onions till golden brown. Pound beef slices to tenderize, brush with oil and either fry or grill them "rare" and tender. Arrange sauerkraut in center of large platter and place roast beef on top. Top with fried onions. Circle platter with Spätzle (recipe see page 184). Serve gravy from frying meat separately.

Sweet Pea Soup with Shrimps

Lower Saxony

When we say "sweet pea" we mean the lissome climber plant, the one with the appetizing appearance and alluring freshness. Served with crayfish or shrimp the color composition is simply irresistible. Ever tried it?

1 lb. sweet peas
2 1/2 cups hot chicken broth
3 tbsp. cream
3 tbsp. butter
salt
white pepper, freshly ground
8 shrimps, fresh
or 8 live fresh-water crayfish
1 pinch sugar
dill seed

Slowly boil whole sweet peas (pod and all) in chicken broth four minutes. Purée everything in blender, strain and heat. Add cream, butter, salt and pepper. Boil shrimps or crayfish with sugar and dill seed 10 minutes. (If you use crayfish, cut off tails and peel.) Serve soup in pre-heated plates, garnish with shrimp or crayfish tails.

Tutti Frutti

Rhineland

Tutti frutti (Italian for "all fruits") did not originate in Italy. It is one of Germany's favorite desserts and the answer to British Trifle. It is one of those recipes which daughters from the upper classes used to bring home from boarding school in their hand-written cookbooks. Tutti Frutti originally was only the medley of fruits from the annual rum crock, the Rumtopf. It wasn't until later that lady fingers and custard crème were added to this Elysian delight.

1 package lady fingers
1 tbsp. rum
1/2 to 1 lb. assorted fruits, either fresh, boiled or best from the rum crock
2 1/2 cups milk
1 package vanilla-flavored sugar or 1 tsp. vanilla extract
4 tbsp. granulated sugar
1 pinch salt
1 1/4 cups milk
4 tbsp. cornstarch
4 egg yolks
1 tbsp. grated almonds
For topping:
3 egg whites
1 package vanilla-flavored sugar or 1 tsp. vanilla extract
1 cup confectioner's sugar

Line heat-resistant bowl with lady fingers and sprinkle with rum. Place fruit on lady fingers. In a pan bring large part of milk to boil, add vanilla, sugar and salt. Meanwhile, in a small bowl mix remaining milk, starch, egg yolks, almonds and stir into slow-boiling milk. Stir thoroughly until mix has consistency of custard. Now pour custard over fruit and lady fingers in bowl. For the **topping**, beat egg whites very stiff, adding vanilla and confectioner's sugar. Heap on top of bowl and place it in pre-heated oven at between 400° to 480°F (200°–250°C) for 10 to 15 minutes. Serve when cool.

Wine Soup

Rhineland

Plutarch, the great Greek philosopher once wrote: "wine, among all the beverages is the most useful, the most tasteful among the medicines and the most pleasant among all the nourishments". Greeks and Romans alike, who never drank their much heavier wines undiluted and hardly without lacing them with spices, also knew how to use wine in the kitchen. Many recipes by the Roman gourmet Marcus Gavius Apicius from the first century AD prove this. What would be more natural than using the wines from the Rhine or Moselle valleys for this recipe, the wines which the Romans savored so much.

3 1/4 cups white wine
juice of one lemon
6 egg yolks
3 whole eggs
sugar to taste
1 package vanilla-flavored sugar or 1 tsp. vanilla extract
8 slices of zwieback
1 tbsp. dried red currant, if desired

Quickly boil wine. Add lemon juice, egg yolks. Beat whole eggs with fork and slowly add them to wine while constantly stirring with mixer at medium speed until soup appears foamy. Add sugar and vanilla. It depends on how dry or sweet the wine originally was when choosing the amount of sugar. Pour soup over zwieback in bowl and serve. If desired, dried red currants can be added, but they should be soaked in cold water one hour before and dried off before adding to soup.

Recipes Classified by Groups

Unless otherwise indicated,
all recipes are for four servings.

Casseroles, Patés and Salty Pies
Bavarian Baked Meat Loaf   16
Black Forest Cherry Casserole   24
Casserole of Asparagus   34
Chicken Paté   40
Onion Pie   122
Paté du Chasseur   128
Pike and Cheese Soufflé   130
Rüdesheim Apple Casserole   166
Sauerkraut Casserole   174
Schales   178

Snacks
Bavarian Baked Meat Loaf   16
Camembert Cheese Spread   32
Casserole of Asparagus   34
Chicken Paté   40
Filled Eggs à la Cologne   64
Grandma's L'il Old Fillet of Herring   84
Fillet Rolls of Matjes on Apple Rings   110
Parfait of Broccoli   124
Paté du Chasseur   128
Ragout of Veal   150
Shrimp Cocktail Husum   182

Fruit Dishes and Desserts
Apples in Morning Gown   14
Black Forest Cherry Casserole   24
Blushing Virgin   28
Red Grits Pudding   154
Rüdesheim Apple Casserole   166
Rum Custard   168
Tutti Frutti   200
Wine Soup   202

Pies, Cakes and Cookies
Apples in Morning Gown   14
Black Forest Cherry Cake   22
Crème of Wine Cake   48
East Frisian Butter Cake   54
Frankfurter Kranz   74
Henrietta's Bridal Cake   88
Hilda Cookies   90
Munich Royal Regent's Cake   114
Nuremberg Ginger Bread   118
Onion Pie   122
Prune Pie   142
Red Current Pie   152
Schneckennudeln   180

Drinks
Egg Nog à la Frisia   60
Elderberry "Champagne"   62
May Wine   112

Recipes in Alphabetical Order

Unless otherwise indicated,
all recipes are for four servings.

References of Photographs

Rainer Kiedrowski and Lieselotte Bergmann 11 u. r.
Kinkelin / Otto Ziegler 8
laenderpress / Mader 13
Löbl-Schreyer 7
Bildarchiv Schuster / Kinne 2
Sirius Bildarchiv / Hans Joachim Döbbelin 14–203
Sirius Bildarchiv / Peter Mueck 11 o., 11 u. l.